MARTIN
STOREY'S

EASY

CABLE

& ARAN

KNITS

MARTIN
STOREY'S

EASY

CABLE

& ARAN

KNITS

26 projects
with a modern
twist

Photography by
Steven Wooster

TS

TRAFALGAR SQUARE
North Pomfret, Vermont

**Martin Storey's Easy Cable &
Aran Knits**

First published in the United States of
America in 2018 by
Trafalgar Square Books
North Pomfret, Vermont 05053

Designs copyright © 2017 Martin Storey
Copyright © 2017 Berry & Co
(Publishing) Ltd

ISBN: 978-1-57076-897-2

Library of Congress Control Number:
2018948385

Design **Steven Wooster**
Pattern writing and knitting **Penny Hill**,
Frances Jago and **Martin Storey**
Pattern checking **Jill Gray** and
Marilyn Wilson
Charts **Steve Jacobson** and
Anne Wilson
Styling **Susan Berry**

Printed in China
10 9 8 7 6 5 4 3 2 1

CONTENTS

INTRODUCTION

As those of you familiar with my knitwear designs will know, cables are my thing – in part because of their history in traditional Aran knitting patterns, but mostly because they create really interesting stitch texture in so many ways. You can play almost endlessly with the variations. But, and this is what surprises people, cables are not actually difficult to knit. You just need to understand the basic principle: you are twisting a set number of stitches across another set number of stitches in a repeating pattern of rows to create a raised pattern. Once you master the basics, the world, as they say, is your oyster!

I created the designs in this book primarily for people who have mastered the basics of knitting and are now ready to move onto easy garments, accessories and home decor with more interesting stitches. To this end, I have created simple shaped garments with interesting cable panels or edgings, as well as cabled items without shaping, such as fingerless mittens, a cowl, a pillow and a throw. As the choice of yarn is so important to the way the cable texture looks, I have chosen Rowan Hemp Tweed and Rowan Softyak DK, as the firm ply of each shows off the cable pattern to best advantage.

I have divided the book into two sections. The first one, **Cable Knits**, concentrates on basic cables that cross knit stiches over knit stitches, mostly on a reversed stockinette stitch background. Although the size and style of these cables varies, the knitting process is very similar, and the abbreviations and symbols used in the patterns are easy to master. If you are knitting cables for the first time, you need to practice, so I have included three very basic cable patterns at the start of the section before launching into the more complex designs. The second section, **Aran**

Knits, takes you to the next level, where you are mastering cable designs that not only cross knit over purl stitches but where several different types of
cable are combined in one panel. Again, I have kicked off the section with three very basic Aran designs for you to practice before continuing with the gallery and patterns for rest of the Aran designs.

We chose to photograph the Cable Knits projects in the beautiful landscape of the Dordogne in France – a stone's throw from where the historic cave paintings were first discovered – which seemed a wholly appropriate location for the cable knits in this book: luminous, light and natural, it had just the ambience we wanted for a collection of designs that are easy to knit, easy to wear and timeless in style. For the second section of the book, **Aran Knits**, we photographed the projects in my home town of Ilfracombe on the north Devon coast. The seaside context references the history of Aran patterns, which originated on the Aran Isles off the west coast of Ireland. These beautiful patterns were used in the local fisherman's sweaters, knitted from the wool of the island's sheep, and with some very intricate and beautiful cable stitch designs, which have since become popularly known as "Aran".

I do hope you enjoy knitting the different designs in this book and that, in doing so, you increase your repertoire of stitch patterns and your understanding of how cable patterns work, perhaps with the end result that you create some fabulous new designs of your own for scarves, wraps, throws and pillows!

At long last I have a website, **www.martinstorey.co.uk**, via which I hope to keep everybody updated on all things new in my world of knitting!

CABLE KNITS

I created the 13 designs in this section
primarily for people who have mastered the
basics of knitting and are now ready to move
into designs with more interesting stitches.
To this end, I have designed some simple
shaped garments with interesting cable panels
or edgings, as well as cabled items without
shaping, such as fingerless mittens, a cowl, a
pillow and a throw. As the choice of yarn is so
important to the way the cable texture looks,
I have chosen Rowan Hemp Tweed, which not
only shows off the cables to best advantage
but, being a thicker yarn, is quicker to knit up.
The first three patterns in this section are
especially chosen as "introductory" designs
and patterns for novice cable knitters,
followed by a gallery of further cable designs
and then their patterns.

WRISTWARMERS *

These wristwarmers make a good starter cable project as they have two different but simple cables: a central 6-st cable back (C6B), flanked by two 4-st cables back and front (C4B and C4F) on each side of it, on a reversed stock-inette stitch background. The pattern is given in chart form, showing the 12-row repeat (see page 123 for reading a chart).

SIZE
To fit average-size hand.

YARN
1 x 1¾oz/50g ball of Rowan Hemp Tweed Almond 141. CYCA#4

NEEDLES
Pair of size 6 (4mm) and size 7 (4.5mm) needles.
Cable needle.

GAUGE
19 sts and 25 rows to 4in/10cm square over st st using size 7 (4.5mm) needles.

ABBREVIATIONS
C4B Slip next 2 sts on a cable needle and leave at back of work, k2, then k2 from cable needle.
C4F Slip next 2 sts on a cable needle and leave at front of work, k2, then k2 from cable needle.
C6B Slip next 3 sts on a cable needle and leave at back of work, k3, then k3 from cable needle.
See also page 127.

LEFT AND RIGHT WRISTWARMERS [BOTH ALIKE]
Using size 6 (4mm) needles, cast on 56 sts, leaving a long enough tail for sewing up.
Rib row 1 (RS) P3, * k2, p2, rep from * to last stitch, p1.
Rib row 2 K3, * p2, k2, rep from * to last stitch, k1.
Rep these 2 rows twice.
Change to size 7 (4.5mm) needles and work in patt from Chart.
Chart row 1 (RS) P5 * k4, p2, k6, p2, k4 * p10; rep from * to * p5.
Chart row 2 K5, * p4, k2, p6, k2, p4, * k10, rep from * to k5.
These 2 rows set the Chart for the 12-row patt rep.
Cont in patt from Chart row 3 to end of Chart row 12.
Now rep rows 1 to 12 from Chart once more, then rows 1 to 4 from Chart

10

KEY
☐ K on RS, P on WS
◼ P on RS, K on WS
C4B
C4F
C6B

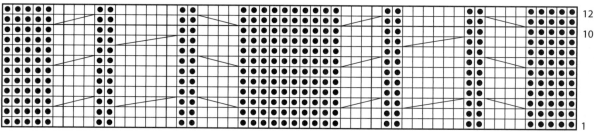

56 sts

once, ending with a wrong side row.
Change to size 6 (4mm) needles.
Now rep Rib rows 1 and 2 three times.
Bind off in patt.

FINISHING
Sew sides together using mattress stitch, leaving a 1½in (3.5cm) gap for the thumb,
3½in (9cm) up from the bottom, cast-on edge.

CABLE PROJECT 2 SCARF*

This scarf has a 10-stitch cable (i.e. crossing 5 knit stitches over 5 knit stitches) with a 20-row repeat. It is knitted on a background of reversed stockinette stitch, with a border of 10 garter stitches at each side edge. The pattern is given in chart form (see page 123 for reading a chart).

SIZE
Scarf measures approx 6in (15cm) x 67in (170cm).

YARN
4 x 1¾oz/50g balls of Rowan Hemp Tweed Kelp 142. CYCA#4

NEEDLES
Pair of size 7 (4.5mm) needles.
Cable needle.

GAUGE
19 sts and 25 rows to 4in/10cm square over st st using size 7 (4.5mm) needles.

ABBREVIATIONS
C10F Slip next 5 sts on a cable needle and leave at front of work, k5, then k5 from cable needle.
C10B Slip next 5 sts on a cable needle and leave at back of work, k5, then k5 from cable needle.
Sl1p ytf Slip one stitch purlwise with yarn in front of work.
See also page 127.

NOTE
In the Chart, a cable symbol going over more than 8 sts is shown as two slashed symbols (over the required number of squares to represent each st).

SCARF
Using size 7 (4.5mm) needles cast on 34 sts and work in patt from Chart.
Chart row 1 (RS) Sl1p ytf, k9, p2, k10, p2, k10.
Chart row 2 Sl1p ytf, k11, p10, k12.
These 2 rows set the Chart for the 20-row patt repeat.
Cont in patt from Chart row 3 to end of Chart row 20.
Now rep rows 1 to 20 from Chart, until Scarf measures approx 67in (170cm), ending on patt row 18 (WS) .
Bind off in patt.

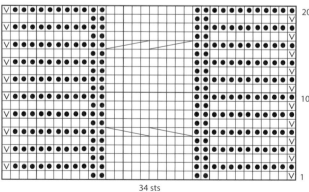

KEY

☐ K on RS, P on WS

● P on RS, K on WS

Ⅴ sl1p ytf on RS and WS

⬜⬜⬜⬜ C10B

⬜⬜⬜⬜ C10F

34 sts

PILLOW *

The plait cable for this pillow is worked over 12 sts with a 16-row repeat. It is knitted on a background of reversed stockinette stitch. The remaining front and back part of the pillow are all in stockinette stitch. The pattern is given in chart form (see page 123 for reading a chart).

SIZE
Pillow measures 12in x 12in (30cm x 30cm).

YARN
2 x 1¾oz/50g balls of Rowan Hemp Tweed Pumice 138. CYAC#4

NEEDLES
Pair of size 6 (4mm) and size 7 (4.5mm) needles.
Cable needle.

EXTRAS
12in x 12in/30cm x 30cm (pillow form.

GAUGE
19 sts and 25 rows to 4in/10cm square over st st using size 7 (4.5mm) needles.

ABBREVIATIONS
C12B Slip next 6 sts on a cable needle and leave at back of work, k6, then k6 from cable needle.
C12F Slip next 6 sts on a cable needle and leave at front of work, k6, then k6 from cable needle.
See also page 127.

PILLOW FRONT
Using size 7 (4.5mm) needles cast on 67 sts.
Work in patt from Chart.
Chart row 1 (RS) K35, work across Row 1 of 22-st rep of Chart, k10.
Chart row 2 P10, work across Row 2 of 22-st rep of Chart, p35.
These 2 rows set the chart and st st for the 16-row patt repeat.
Cont in patt from Chart row 3 to end of Chart row 16.
Now rep rows 1 to 16 from Chart, 3 more times, then rows 1 to 14 from Chart once, ending with a WS row.
Bind off in patt.

PILLOW BACK
Using size 7 (4.5mm) needles cast on 59 sts.
Beg with a k row, cont in st st for 78 rows.
Bind off.

FINISHING
With wrong sides together, sew back to front along 3 sides using mattress stitch. Insert the pillow form and join rem seam.

KEY

☐ K on RS, P on WS

⦿ P on RS, K on WS

C12B

C12F

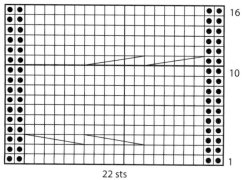

22 sts

TENDRIL CABLE SCARF

Super-sized cables are perfect for a very simple, extra long scarf, which can be
joined at each end so it can be worn looped several times around the neck,
as shown here. This elongated plait design is knitted in Rowan Hemp Tweed.
Pattern on page 54.

CHAIN CABLE SLIPOVER

This neat little slipover is perfect for layering over a printed dress or shirt. The staghorn cable panel on the front and back is bordered with a right and left twist cable on either side. Knitted in Rowan Hemp Tweed. *Pattern on page 44.*

CORKSCREW CABLE SHAWL

This has just a hint of a cable forming the straight edge of the triangular shawl
and a long tail that can be knotted or looped around, with a fringe at each end.
Knitted in Rowan Hemp Tweed. *Pattern on page 42.*

CABLE EDGE JACKET

This is another simply constructed garment with drop shoulders and a boxy shape; the cuffs of the short sleeves and the front bands are each decorated with the same simple cable. It can be worn dressed up, or dressed down with jeans. Knitted in Rowan Hemp Tweed. *Pattern on page 38.*

WOODLAND CABLE BLANKET

It is fun to have a simple patched project on the go. This pretty little blanket has
an alternating lacy tree and leaf design for each of the patches, and the assembled
blanket is trimmed with a rope cable edging. Knitted in Rowan Hemp Tweed.

Pattern on page 62.

GARTER TWIST COWL

This cowl is a great first-time cable project, as it has no shaping. The same alternating stockinette stitch and garter stitch cable pattern repeats around the cowl, with a deep rib at the top and bottom. Knitted in Rowan Hemp Tweed.

Pattern on page 46.

LINKS CABLE CARDIGAN

A classic V-neck, longer length cardigan is made special with a cable panel bordering the button band on the left and right fronts. Knitted in Rowan Hemp Tweed. *Pattern on page 48.*

SEED TWIST MITTENS

This is another great introductory cable knit project with its interesting textural
stitch variation to the simple cable panel on the back of the fingerless mittens.
Knitted in Rowan Hemp Tweed. *Pattern on page 52.*

WAVE CABLE CARDIGAN

The narrow cable panel on this elegant short cardigan is simple but very effective.
The cardigan design is enhanced by the garter-stitch yoke front and back,
and the simple rolled garter-stitch collar. Knitted in Rowan Hemp Tweed.

Pattern on page 56.

WINDOWPANE PILLOW

This small seed-stitch and simple repeating cable design
is used for two identical pillows in toning colorways. The
back of each pillow is seed stitch only. *Pattern on page 60.*

CABLE PATTERNS

When knitting a cable pattern, you must take care to look at the abbreviations carefully before you start, to make sure you understand exactly what you are doing. Each pattern carries its own special abbreviations, but there is also a list of general abbreviations used in the book on page 127.

The patterns for the fitted garments include a range of sizes with their actual measurements (ie with ease) for the bust sizes given.

Generally the patterns without shaping (marked *) will be the best ones to work on if you are a novice cable knitter, unless you are already familiar with knitting to the correct gauge to get a garment to fit. It is essential to work to the gauge provided (and to change the needles to a size larger or smaller if your knitting is respectively too tight or too loose). See pages 122-7 for further notes on working to gauge and for an explanation of * ratings.

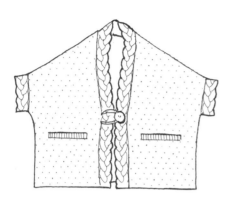

CABLE EDGE JACKET*

To fit bust

36-38	40-42	44-46	48-50	in
92-97	102-107	112-117	122-127	cm

Finished measurements

Bust

50½	55	60	66	in
128	140	152	165	cm

Length to back neck

26½	27½	28¾	30	in
67	70	73	76	cm

YARN

12(13:15:16) x 1¾oz/50g balls
Rowan Hemp Tweed Duck Egg
139. CYCA#4

NEEDLES

Pair each size 6 (4mm) and size 7
(4.5mm) knitting needles.
Circular size 6 (4mm) and size 7
(4.5mm) knitting needles.
Cable needle.

GAUGE

19 sts and 25 rows to 4in/10cm
square over st st using size 7
(4.5mm) needles.

38

ABBREVIATIONS

C8B Slip next 4 sts on a cable
needle, hold at back of work, k4,
then k4 from cable needle.
C8F Slip next 4 sts on a cable
needle, hold at front of work, k4,
then k4 from cable needle.
See also page 127.

BACK

With size 6 (4mm) circular needle, cast on 123(135:147:159) sts.
Work backwards and forwards in rows.
K 6 rows.
Change to size 7 (4.5mm) circular needle and patt as foll:
Row 1 (RS) K to end.
Row 2 P to end.
Row 3 K3, [p1, k3] to end.
Row 4 P to end.
Row 5 K to end.
Row 6 P to end.
Row 7 K1, [p1, k3] to last 2 sts, p1, k1.
Row 8 P to end.
These 8 rows form the patt and are repeated throughout.
Cont in patt until back measures 13¾(14:14½:15)in/35(36:37:38)cm from
cast-on edge ending with a WS row.
Armhole border
Row 1 Cast on 13 sts, k these 13 sts, then patt to end.
Row 2 Cast on 13 sts, k3, p7, k3, patt to last 13 sts, k3, p7, k3.
149(161:173:185) sts.
Row 3 K13, patt to last 13 sts, k13.
Row 4 K3, p2, [m1, p1] 5 times, k3, patt to last 13 sts, k3, p2, [m1, p1] 5
times, k3. *159(171:183:195) sts.*
Cont in cable patt.
Row 1 Work Row 1 of Chart, patt to last 18 sts.
Row 2 Work Row 2 of Chart, patt to last 18 sts.
These 2 rows set the 12-row, 18-st cable panel at each end of the row.
Cont in patt until back measures 23(23½:24½:25¼)in/58(60:62:64)cm from
cast-on edge ending with a right side row.
Next row K3, p2, [p2tog] 5 times, k3, patt to last 18 sts, k3, p2, [p2tog] 5
times, k3. *149(161:173:185) sts.*
Shape shoulder
Bind off 13 sts at beg of next 2 rows. *123(135:147:159) sts.*

Bind off 6 sts at beg of next 20(22:24:26) rows. *3 sts.*
Work 3tog and fasten off.

Pocket linings (both alike)
Using size 7 (4.5mm) needles cast on 30(34:34:38) sts.
Beg with a k row, work 30(32:34:36) rows in st st.
Leave these sts on a holder.

LEFT FRONT

With size 6 (4mm) needles cast on 72(78:84:90) sts.
K 6 rows.
Change to size 7 (4.5mm) needles and patt.
Row 1 (RS) K to end.
Row 2 K3, p2, [m1, p1] 5 times, k3, for cable border, p to end. *77(83:89:95) sts.*
Row 3 K3(5:3:5), [p1, k3] to last 18 sts, k18.
Row 4 K3, p12, k3, p to end.
Row 5 K to last 18 sts, k3, C8B, k7.
Row 6 K3, p12, k3, p to end.
Row 7 K1(3:1:3), [p1, k3] to last 20 sts, p1, k19.
Row 8 K3, p12, k3, p to end.
These 8 rows form the main patt and the first 6 rows of the cable panel.
Work rows 7 to 12 from Chart, then repeat the 12 rows **at the same time** work a further 24(26:28:30) rows.

Place pocket
Next row Patt 16(18:24:26), place next 30(34:34:38) sts on a holder, patt across 30(34:34:38) sts of pocket lining, patt to end.
Cont in patt until front measures 13¾(14:14½:15)in/35(36:37:38)cm from cast-on edge ending with a wrong side row.

Armhole border
Row 1 Cast on 13 sts, k these 13 sts, then patt to end.
Row 2 Patt to last 13 sts, k3, p7, k3. *90(96:102:108) sts.*
Row 3 K13, patt to end.
Row 4 Patt to last 13 sts, k3, p2, [m1, p1] 5 times, k3. *95(101:107:113) sts.*
Cont in cable patt.
Row 1 Work Row 1 of Chart, patt to end.
Row 2 Patt to last 18 sts, work Row 2 of Chart.
These 2 rows set the cable panel for armhole border.
Cont in patt until front measures 23(23½:24½:25¼)in/58(60:62:64)cm from cast-on edge, ending with a right side row.
Next row Patt to last 18 sts, k3, p2, [p2tog] 5 times, k3. *90(96:102:108) sts.*

Shape shoulder
Next row Bind off 13 sts, patt to end. *77(83:89:95) sts.*
Patt 1 row.
Bind off 6 sts at beg of next and 9(10:11:12) foll right side rows. *17 sts.*
Next row K3, p2, [p2tog] 5 times, k2. *12 sts.*
Bind off.

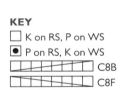

KEY
☐ K on RS, P on WS
▣ P on RS, K on WS
C8B
C8F

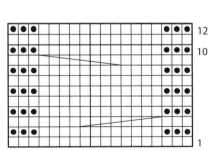

18 sts

RIGHT FRONT

With size 6 (4mm) needles cast on 72(78:84:90) sts.

K 6 rows.

Change to size 7 (4.5mm) needles and patt.

Row 1 (RS) K to end.

Row 2 P59(65:71:77), k3, p2, [m1, p1] 5 times, k3, for cable border. *77(83:89:95) sts.*

Row 3 K18, for border, [k3,p1] to last 3(5:3:5)sts, k3(5:3:5).

Row 4 P to last 18 sts, k3, p12, k3.

Row 5 K3, C8B, k to end.

Row 6 P to last 18 sts, k3, p12, k3.

Row 7 K19, p1, [k3, p1] to last 1(3:1:3)sts, k1(3:1:3).

Row 8 P to last 18 sts, k3, p12, k3.

These 8 rows form the main patt and the first 6 rows of the cable panel. Work rows 7 to 12 from Chart, then repeat the 12 rows, **at the same time** work a further 24(26:28:30) rows.

Place pocket

Next row Patt 31, place next 30(34:34:38) sts on a holder, patt across 30(34:34:38) sts of pocket lining, patt to end.

Cont in patt until front measures 13¾(14:14½:15)in/35(36:37:38)cm from cast-on edge, ending with a right side row.

Armhole border

Row 1 Cast on 13 sts, k3, p7, k3, patt to end. *90(96:102:108) sts.*

Row 2 Patt to last 13sts, k13.

Row 3 K3, p2, [m1, p1] 5 times, k3, patt to end. *95(101:107:113) sts.*

Cont in cable patt.

Row 1 Patt to last 18 sts, work Row 1 of Chart.

Row 2 Work Row 2 of Chart, patt to end.

These 2 rows set the cable panel for armhole border.

Cont in patt until front measures 23(23½:24½:25¼)in/58(60:62:64)cm from cast-on edge ending with a right side row.

Next row K3, p2, [p2tog] 5 times, k3, patt to end. *90(96:102:108) sts.*

Patt 1 row.

Shape shoulder

Next row Bind off 13 sts, patt to end. *77(83:89:95) sts.*

Patt 1 row.

Bind off 6 sts at beg of next and 8(9:10:11) foll wrong side rows. *17 sts.*

Patt 1 row.

Next row Bind off 6 sts, k next st, p2, [p2tog] 5 times, k3. *12 sts.*

Bind off.

POCKET TOPS (both alike)

With right side facing, using 4mm (US 6) needles, place sts on a needle.

Row 1 K4, [p2, k2] to last 6 sts, p2, k4.

Row 2 K2, [p2, k2] to end.

Rep the last 2 rows twice more.

Bind off in rib.

FINISHING

Join shoulder seams. Join bound-off edges of front bands. Join side and cast-on edges of armbands. Sew down pocket linings and pocket tops.

CORKSCREW CABLE SHAWL*

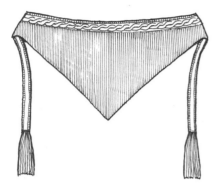

SIZE
16½in (42cm) at widest part.

YARN
7 x 1¾oz/50g balls of Rowan Hemp Tweed Kelp 142. CYCA#4

NEEDLES
Pair each size 6 (4mm) and size 7 (4.5mm) knitting needles.
Cable needle.

EXTRAS
2 eyelets

42

GAUGE
19 sts and 34 rows to 4in/10cm square over st st using size 7 (4.5mm) needles.

ABBREVIATIONS
C8B Slip next 4 sts on a cable needle and leave at back of work, k4, then k4 from cable needle.
See also page 127.

TO MAKE
Using size 6 (4mm) needles cast on 11 sts.
Row 1 K1, [yf, k2tog] 5 times.
Row 2 Sl 1, k to end.
Rep the last row 4 times more.
Change to size 7 (4.5mm) needles.
Next row Sl 1, k to end.
Inc row Sl 1, k3, [p1, m1] 3 times, k4. *14 sts.*
Work in cable patt.
Row 1 Sl 1, k13.
Row 2 Sl 1, k2, p8, k3.
Rows 3 and 4 As rows 1 and 2.
Row 5 Sl 1, k2, C8B, k3.
Row 6 As row 2.
Rows 7 to 10 Rep rows 1 and 2 twice.
These 10 rows form the cable panel.
Work a further 80 rows, ending with a 10th row.
Shape side
Row 1 (RS) Sl 1, patt to end.
Row 2 Sl 1, patt to end.
Row 3 Sl 1, patt to end.
Row 4 Sl 1, k1, inc in next st, patt to end. *15 sts.*
Rows 5 to 296 Working inc sts into g-st, rep the last 4 rows 73 times. *88 sts.*
Row 297 (RS) Sl 1, patt to end.
Row 298 Sl 1, patt to end.
Row 299 Sl 1, patt to end.
Row 300 Sl 1, k1, k2tog, patt to end. *87 sts.*
Rows 301 to 592 Rep the last 4 rows 73 times. *14 sts.*
Work 89 rows in patt, ending row 1.
Next row Sl 1, k2, p1, [p2tog] 3 times, p1, k3. *11 sts.*
Change to size 6 (4mm) needles.
Next row Sl 1, k to end.
Rep the last row 5 times more.
Next row K1, [yf, k2tog] 5 times.
Bind off.

FINISHING
Cut forty 24in (60cm) lengths of yarn. Knot 4 lengths through each eyelet at each end.

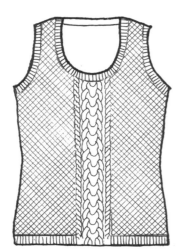

YARN

6(7:7:8) × 1¾oz/50g balls of
Rowan Hemp Tweed Almond 141.
CYCA#4

NEEDLES

Pair each size 5 (3.75mm) and
size 7 (4.5mm) knitting needles.
Cable needle.

GAUGE

20 sts and 25 rows to 4in/10cm
square over seed st using size 5
(3.75mm) needles.

44

ABBREVIATIONS

C4F Slip next 2 sts on a cable
needle and hold at front of work,
k2, then k2 from cable needle.
C4B Slip next 2 stitches on a cable
needle and hold at back of work,
k2, then k2 from cable needle.
C6F Slip next 3 sts on a cable
needle and hold at front of work,
k3, then k3 from cable needle.
C6B Slip next 3 stitches on a cable
needle and hold at back of work,
k3, then k3 from cable needle.
See also page 127.

CHAIN CABLE SLIPOVER**

To fit bust

32-34	36-38	40-42	44-46	in
82-86	92-97	102-107	112-117	cm

Finished measurements

Bust

34¾	39½	44	48¾	in
88	100	112	124	cm

Length to back neck

20½	21¼	22	23¾	in
52	54	56	58	cm

BACK

Using size 5 (3.75mm) needles cast on 98(110:122:134) sts.
Rib row 1 P2(0:2:0), [k2, p2] 8(10:11:13) times, k4, p2, [k2, p2] 5 times, k4,
[p2, k2] 8(10:11:13) times, p2(0:2:0).
Rib row 2 K2(0:2:0), [p2, k2] 8 (10:11:13) times, p4, k2, [p2, k2] 5 times, p4,
[k2, p2] 8(10:11:13) times, k2(0:2:0).
Rib row 3 P2(0:2:0), [k2, p2] 8(10:11:13) times, C4B, p2, [k2, p2] 5 times,
C4F, [p2, k2] 8(10:11:13) times, p2(0:2:0).
Rib row 4 K2(0:2:0), [p2, k2] 8(10:11:13) times, p4, k2, [p2, k2] 5 times, p4,
[k2, p2] 8(10:11:13) times, k2(0:2:0).
Rep these 4 rows once more.
Change to size 7 (4.5mm) needles and patt.
Row 1 [K1, p1] 16(19:22:25) times, p2, work across row 1 of cable panel, p2,
[p1, k1] 16(19:22:25) times.
Row 2 [K1, p1] 16(19:22:25) times, k2, work across row 2 of cable panel, k2,
[p1, k1] 16(19:22:25) times.
These 2 rows form the seed st and set the cable panel position.
Dec row Seed st to 3 sts before cable panel, p2tog, p1, work across cable
panel, p1, p2tog, seed st to end.
Patt 5 rows as set.
Rep the last 6 rows 3 times more and the Dec row again.
Work 9 row straight.
Inc row Seed st to 2 sts before cable panel, m1, p2, work across cable
panel, p2, m1, seed st to end.
Rep the last 10 rows 4 times more.
Cont in patt until work measures 12¼(12½:13:13¼)in/31(32:33:34)cm from
cast-on edge, ending with a wrong side row.
Shape armholes
Bind off 7(9:11:13) sts at beg of next 2 rows. *84(92:100:108) sts.*
Next row Skpo, patt to last 2 sts, k2tog.
Next row Patt to end.
Rep the last 2 rows 6(7:8:9) times more. *70(76:82:88) sts **.*

Cont straight until Back measures 19¾(20½:21¼:22)in/50(52:54:56)cm from cast-on edge, ending with a wrong side row.

Shape shoulders and back neck

Next row Patt 15(17:19:21), turn and work on these sts for first side of back neck.

Dec one st at neck edge on next 3 rows. 12(14:16:18) sts.

Shape shoulder

Bind off.

With right side facing, place center 40(42:44:46) sts on a spare needle, rejoin yarn to rem sts, patt to end.

Dec one st at neck edge on next 3 rows. 12(14:16:18) sts.

Patt 1 row.

Shape shoulder

Bind off.

FRONT

Work as given for Back to **.

Shape front neck

Next row Patt 22(24:26:28) sts, turn and work on these sts for first side of neck shaping.

Dec one st at neck edge on every right side row until 12(14:16:18) sts rem. Work straight until front measures the same as back to shoulder, ending at armhole edge.

Shape shoulder

Bind off.

With right side facing, place center 26(28:30:32) sts on a spare needle, rejoin yarn to rem sts, patt to end.

Dec one st at neck edge on every right side row until 12(14:16:18) sts rem. Work straight until front measures the same as back to shoulder, ending at armhole edge.

Patt 1 row.

Shape shoulder

Bind off.

NECKBAND

Join right shoulder seam.

With right side facing using size 5 (3.75mm) needles pick up and k32(34:36:38) sts down left side of front neck, decreasing 8 sts, patt 26(28:30:32) sts from front neck holder, pick up and k32(34:36:38) sts up right side of front neck, 3 sts down right side of back neck, decreasing 10 sts, patt 40(42:44:46) sts from back neck holder, pick up and k3 sts up left side of back neck. *118(126:134:142) sts.*

Rib row 1 K2, [p2, k2] to end.

Rib row 2 P2, [k2, p2] to end.

Rib row 3 K2, [p2, k2] to end.

Bind off in rib.

ARMBANDS

Join left shoulder and neckband seam.

With right side facing, using size 5 (3.75mm) needles, pick up and k98(102:106:110) sts evenly round armhole edge.

Work 3 rows rib as given for neckband.

Bind off in rib.

FINISHING

Join side and armband seams.

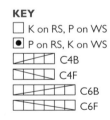

45

KEY

☐ K on RS, P on WS
◉ P on RS, K on WS
C4B
C4F
C6B
C6F

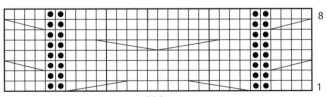

30 sts

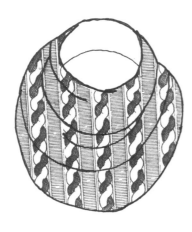

GARTER TWIST COWL*

TO MAKE

Using size 6 (4mm) circular needle cast on 156 sts.
Taking care not to twist the sts, work in rounds.
Next round * [P2, k3] twice, [p2, k2] 4 times; rep from * 5 times.
Rep this round 9 times more.
Change to size 7 (4.5mm) circular needle and work in patt from Chart.
Round 1 [Work across Round 1 of 26-st patt rep] 6 times.
This round sets the 12-round patt repeat.
Work a further 59 rounds.
Next round * [P2, k3] twice, [p2, k2] 4 times; rep from * 5 times.
Rep this round 9 times more.
Bind off in rib.

SIZE

26in (66cm) circumference;
11in (28cm) deep.

YARN

3 x 1¾oz/50g balls of Rowan Hemp
Tweed Pumice 138. CYCA#4

NEEDLES

Size 6 (4mm) and size 7 (4.5mm)
circular knitting needles,
24in/60cm long.
Cable needle.

GAUGE

19 sts and 25 rows to 4in/10cm
square over st st using size 7
(4.5mm) needle.

ABBREVIATIONS

C8B Slip next 4 sts on a cable
needle and leave at back of work,
k4, then k4 from cable needle.
See also page 127.

NOTE

When working from Chart all rows
are right side rows and read from
right to left.

46

KEY

☐ K on RS, P on WS

● P on RS, K on WS

▱ C8B

26-st rep

12
10

1

LINKS CABLE CARDIGAN**

To fit bust

| 36-38 | 40-42 | 44-46 | 48-50 | in |
| 92-97 | 102-107 | 112-117 | 122-127 | cm |

Finished measurements

Bust

| 42½ | 47¾ | 52½ | 57½ | in |
| 108 | 121 | 133 | 146 | cm |

Length to Back neck

| 26 | 26¾ | 27½ | 28½ | in |
| 66 | 68 | 70 | 72 | cm |

Sleeve length
17¼in/44cm

YARN
12(13:15:16) x 1¾oz/50g balls
Rowan Hemp Tweed Kelp 142.
CYCA#4

NEEDLES
Pair each size 6 (4mm) and size 7
(4.5mm) knitting needles.
Cable needle.

GAUGE
19 sts and 25 rows to 4in/10cm
square over st st using size 7
(4.5mm) needles.

48

EXTRAS
Six buttons

ABBREVIATIONS
C4F Slip next 2 sts on a cable
needle and hold at front of work,
k2, then k2 from cable needle.
C4B Slip next 2 stitches on a cable
needle and hold at back of work,
k2, then k2 from cable needle.
C6F Slip next 3 sts on a cable
needle and hold at front of work,
k3, then k3 from cable needle.
C6B Slip next 3 stitches on a cable
needle and hold at back of work,
k3, then k3 from cable needle.
See also page 127.

BACK
With size 6 (4mm) needles cast on 105(117:129:141) sts.
Row 1 K1, [p1, k1] to end.
Row 2 P1, [k1, p1] to end.
These 2 rows form the rib.
Work a further 24 rows.
Change to size 7 (4.5mm) needles.
Beg with k row work in st st until back measures 24¾(25½:26½:27)in/
63(65:67:69)cm from cast-on edge, ending with a p row.
Shape upper arms
Bind off 7(8:9:10) sts at beg of next 6 rows. *63(69:75:81) sts.*
Shape shoulders
Bind off 13(14:15:16) sts at beg of next 2 rows.
Bind off rem 37(41:45:49) sts.

LEFT FRONT
With size 6 (4mm) needles cast on 58(64:70:76) sts.
Row 1 K1, [p1, k1] to last 3 sts, p1, k2.
Row 2 [K1, p1] to end.
These 2 rows form the rib.
Work a further 16 rows.
Change to size 7 (4.5mm) needles.
Row 1 K to last 31 sts, work across Row 1 of Left front Chart, turn, cast on
one st, leave rem 8 sts on a safety pin for front band. *51(57:63:69) sts.*
Row 2 P1, work across Row 2 of Chart, p to end.
Row 3 K to last 24 sts, work across Row 3 of Chart, k1.
These 3 rows set the Cable panel with st st to the side.
Cont in patt until 66(70:74:78) rows fewer in st st have been worked than
on Back to Shape upper arms.
Neck shaping
Row 1 K to last 26 sts, k2tog, patt 24.
Patt 3 rows.

Left front

23 sts

Right front

23 sts

KEY

☐ K on RS, P on WS
● P on RS, K on WS
C4B
C4F
C6B
C6F

50

Rep the last 4 rows 12(14:16:18) times and row I again. *37(41:45:49) sts.*
Work 13(9:5:1) rows straight.

Shape upper arm
Decreasing one st over 4-st cable and 2 sts over 13-st cable, cast off 7(8:9:10) sts at beg of next and 2 foll right side rows.
Work I row.

Shape shoulder
Bind off rem 13(14:15:16) sts.

RIGHT FRONT
With size 6 (4mm) needles cast on 58(64:70:76) sts.
Row I K2, [pI, kI] to end
Row 2 [PI, kI] to end.
These 2 rows form the rib.
Work a further 4 rows.
Buttonhole row Rib 3, skpo, yf, rib to end.
Work a further II rows.
Row I Rib 8, leave these sts on a safety pin or front band, then change to size 7 (4.5mm) needle, cast on I st, work across Row I of Right front Chart, k to end. *51(57:63:69) sts.*
Cont with size 7 (4.5mm) needles.
Row 2 P to last 24 sts, work across Row 2 of Chart, pI.
Row 3 KI, work across Row 3 of Chart, k to end.
These 3 rows set the Cable Panel with st st to the side.
Cont in patt until 66(70:74:78) rows fewer have been worked than on Back to Shape upper arms.

Neck shaping
Row I Patt 24, skpo, k to end.

Patt 3 rows.

Rep the last 4 rows 12(14:16:18) times and row 1 again. *37(41:45:49) sts.*

Work 14(10:6:2) rows straight.

Shape upper arm

Decreasing one st over 4-st cable and 2 sts over 13-st cable, bind off
7(8:9:10) sts at beg of next and 2 foll wrong side rows.

Work 1 row.

Shape shoulder

Bind off rem 13(14:15:16) sts.

LEFT FRONT BAND

With right side facing, place sts on a size 6 (4mm) needle, inc in first st, rib to
end. Cont in rib until band fits up left front and halfway across back neck.
Bind off.

Mark position for buttons, the first one on the 7th row of rib, the 6th one 4 rows
below beg of neck shaping, and rem 4 spaced evenly between.

RIGHT FRONT BAND

With wrong side facing, place sts on a size 6 (4mm) needle, inc in first st,
rib to end.

Working buttonholes to match markers, cont in rib until band fits up right
front and halfway across back neck. Bind off.

SLEEVES

With size 6 (4mm) needles cast on 45(49:53:57) sts.

Row 1 K1, [p1, k1] to end.

Row 2 P1, [k1, p1] to end.

These 2 rows form the rib.

Work a further 16 rows.

Change to size 7 (4.5mm) needles.

Beg with a k row, work in st st.

Inc row K4, m1, k to last 4 sts, m1, k4.

Work 3 rows.

Rep the last 4 rows 18 times and the inc row again. *85(89:93:97) sts.*

Cont straight until sleeve measures 17¼in/44cm from cast-on edge, ending
with a wrong side row.

Shape top

Bind off 6 sts at beg of next 10 rows.

Bind off.

BUTTON BAND

Join right shoulder seam.

Bind off in rib.

FINISHING

Join shoulder seams. Sew on front bands and join at center back neck. With
center of sleeve to shoulder seam, sew on sleeves. Join side and sleeve seams.
Sew on buttons.

SEED TWIST MITTENS*

RIGHT MITTEN

With size 6 (4mm) needles cast on 40 sts.
Rib row 1 [K2, p2] 6 times, k4, [k1, p1] twice, [p2, k2] twice.
Rib row 2 [P2, k2] twice, [p1, k1] twice, p4, [k2, p2] 6 times.
Rep these 2 rows twice.
Change to size 7 (4.5mm) needles.
Row 1 [K1, p1] 11 times, p2, slip next 4 sts on cable needle and hold at back of work, [k1, p1] twice, then k4 from cable needle, p2, [p1, k1] 3 times.
Row 2 [K1, p1] 3 times, k2, p4, [p1, k1] twice, k2, [p1, k1] 11 times.
Row 3 [K1, p1] 11 times, p2, [k1, p1] twice, k4, p2, [p1, k1] 3 times.
Row 4 [K1, p1] 3 times, k2, p4, [p1, k1] twice, k2, [p1, k1] 11 times.
Rows 5 to 10 Rep rows 3 and 4 three times.
Row 11 [K1, p1] 11 times, p2, slip next 4 sts on cable needle and hold at back of work, k4, then [k1, p1] twice, from cable needle, p2, [p1, k1] 3 times.
Row 12 [K1, p1] 3 times, k2, [p1, k1] twice, p4, k2, [p1, k1] 11 times.
Row 13 [K1, p1] 11 times, p2, k4, [k1, p1] twice, p2, [p1, k1] 3 times.
Row 14 [K1, p1] 3 times, k2, [p1, k1] twice, p4, k2, [p1, k1] 11 times.
Rows 15 to 20 Rep rows 13 and 14 three times.
** These 20 rows form the cable panel with seed st each side.
Work a further 40 rows, ending with a 20th row of patt.
Thumb shaping
Row 1 Inc in first st, patt to last 2 sts, inc in next st, seed st 1.
Row 2 Patt to end.
Rep the last 2 rows 7 times more. *56 sts.*
Next row Seed st 8, turn.
Work 6 rows in seed st.
Bind off in seed st.
Next row With right side facing, rejoin yarn to next st, patt to end.
Next row Seed st 8, turn.
Work 6 rows in seed st.
Bind off in seed st.
Next row With wrong side facing, rejoin yarn to next st, patt to end. *40 sts.*
Work a further 2 rows in patt, ending with a 20th row of patt.
Change to size 6 (4mm) needles.
Rib row 1 [K2, p2] 6 times, k4, [k1, p1] twice, [p2, k2] twice.
Rib row 2 [P2, k2] twice, [p1, k1] twice, p4, [k2, p2] 6 times.
Rep these 2 rows twice more.
Bind off in patt **.

LEFT MITTEN

With size 6 (4mm) needles cast on 40 sts.
Rib row 1 [K2, p2] twice, k4, [k1, p1] twice, [p2, k2] 6 times.
Rib row 2 [P2, k2] 6 times, [p1, k1] twice, p4, [k2, p2] twice.
Rep these 2 rows twice more.

SIZE
To fit small/medium hands.
Length 11½in (29cm).

YARN
2 x 1¾oz/50g balls Rowan Hemp Tweed Almond 141 CYCA#4

NEEDLES
Pair each size 6 (4mm) and size 7 (4.5mm) needles.
Cable needle.

GAUGE
19 sts and 33 rows to 4in/10cm measured over seed st using size 7 (4.5mm) needles.

ABBREVIATIONS
See also page 127.

52

Change to size 7 (4.5mm) needles.

Row 1 [K1, p1] 3 times, p2, slip next 4 sts on cable needle and hold at back of work, [k1, p1] twice, then k4 from cable needle, p2, [p1, k1] 11 times.

Row 2 [K1, p1] 11 times, k2, p4, [p1, k1] twice, k2, [p1, k1] 3 times.

Row 3 [K1, p1] 3 times, p2, [k1, p1] twice, k4, p2, [p1, k1] 11 times.

Row 4 [K1, p1] 11 times, k2, p4, [p1, k1] twice, k2, [p1, k1] 3 times.

Rows 5 to 10 Rep rows 3 and 4 three times.

Row 11 [K1, p1] 3 times, p2, slip next 4 sts on cable needle and hold at back of work, k4, then [k1, p1] twice, from cable needle, p2, [p1, k1] 11 times.

Row 12 [K1, p1] 11 times, k2, [p1, k1] twice, p4, k2, [p1, k1] 3 times.

Row 13 [K1, p1] 3 times, p2, k4, [k1, p1] twice,p2, [p1, k1] 11 times.

Row 14 [K1, p1] 11 times, k2, [p1, k1] twice, p4, k2, [p1, k1] 3 times.

Rows 15 to 20 Rep rows 13 and 14 three times.

Now work as given for Right Mitten from ** to **.

FINISHING
Join side and thumb seams.

SIZE

Approx 3½in (9in) wide; 98½in (250cm) long.

YARN

5 x 1¾oz/50g balls of Rowan Hemp Tweed Pine 135. CYCA#4

54

NEEDLES

Pair of size 7 (4.5mm) needles. Cable needle.

GAUGE

19 sts and 25 rows to 4in/10cm square over st st using size 7 (4.5mm) needles.

ABBREVIATIONS

C20F Slip next 10 sts on a cable needle and hold at front of work, k10, then k10 from cable needle.
C20B Slip next 10 sts on a cable needle and hold at back of work, k10, then k10 from cable needle.
See also page 127.

TENDRIL CABLE SCARF *

BACK

Using 4.5mm (US 7) needles cast on 24 sts.
Rib row 1 P1, [k2, p2] five times, k2, p1.
Rib row 2 P3, [k2, p2] four times, k2, p3.
These 2 rows form the rib.
Work a further 29 rows.
Inc row P3, [m1, k2, m1, p2] 4 times, m1, k2, m1, p3. *34 sts.*
Work in Cable patt.
Row 1 P2, k30, p2.
Row 2 K2, p30, k2.
Rows 3 and 4 As Rows 1 and 2.
Row 5 P2, C20B, k10, p2.
Row 6 K2, p30, k2.
Rows 7 to 16 Rep Rows 1 and 2 five times.
Row 17 P2, k10, C20F, p2.
Row 18 K2, p30, k2.
Rows 19 to 24 Rep Rows 1 and 2 three times.
These 24 rows form the Cable patt.
Cont in Cable patt until scarf measures approx 94in/238cm from cast-on edge, ending with Row 21.
Next row K2, [p2tog, p1] 10 times, k2. *24 sts.*
Work 31 rows in rib as given at beg.
Bind off in rib.

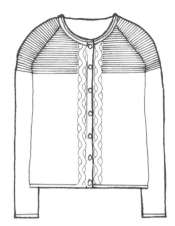

YARN
9(9:10:11:11:12) × 1¾oz/50g balls of Rowan Hemp Tweed Cameo 140. CYCA#4

NEEDLES
Pair each size 6 (4mm) and size 7 (4.5mm) knitting needles.
Cable needle.

GAUGE
19 sts and 25 rows to 4in/10cm square over st st using size 7 (4.5mm) needles.
19 sts and 34 rows to 10cm/4in square over g-st using size 6 (4mm) needles or size to obtain correct gauge

EXTRAS
7 buttons

ABBREVIATIONS
C6F Slip next 3 sts on a cable needle and hold at front of work, k3 then k3 from cable needle;
C6B Slip next 3 stitches on a cable needle and hold at back of work, k3, then k3 from cable needle.
wrap 1 Slip stitch from left to right needle purlwise, bringing yarn to front, place slipped stitch back on left needle.
See also page 127.

WAVE CABLE CARDIGAN**

To fit bust

32	34	36	38	40	42	in
82	86	92	97	102	107	cm

Finished measurements
Bust

34	35¾	37¾	39¾	42	44	in
86	91	96	101	107	112	cm

Length to shoulder

21	21¼	21¾	22	22¾	23¼	in
53	54	55	56	58	59	cm

Sleeve length - all sizes
17¾in (45cm)

BACK
With size 6 (4mm) needles cast on 83(88:93:98:103:108) sts.
K 7 rows.
Change to US 7 (4.5mm) needles.
Beg with a k row, cont in st st until back measures
11½(11½:11¾:11¾:12¼:12¼)in/29(29:30:30:31:31)cm
from cast-on edge, ending with a p row.
Shape raglan armholes
Bind off 4(5:6:7:8:9) sts at beg of next 2 rows. 75(78:81:84:87:90) sts.
Next row K2, skpo, k to last 4 sts, k2 tog, k2.
Next row P to end.
Rep the last 2 rows 6(7:8:9:10:11) times more. 61(62:63:64:65:66) sts.
Change to size 6 (4mm) needles.
Next row K2, skpo, k to last 4 sts, k2 tog, k2.
K 3 rows.
Rep the last 4 rows 14 times. 31(32:33:34:35:36) sts.
Leave these sts on a spare needle.

LEFT FRONT
With size 6 (4mm) needles cast on 45(48:50:53:56:58) sts.
Row 1 (WS) K7, p6, k to end.
Row 2 K to last 15 sts, p2, k6, p2, k5.
Row 3 K7, p6, k to end.
Row 4 K to last 15 sts, p2, C6B, p2, k5.
Row 5 K7, p6, k to end.
Rows 6 and 7 As rows 2 and 3.
Change to size 7 (4.5mm) needles.
Work in patt from Left front Chart.
Row 1 K to last 15 sts, p2, k6, p2 from Chart, k5.
Row 2 K5, then k2, p6, k2 from Chart, p to end.
These 2 rows set the 12-row cable panel and g-st front border with st st body.

Work straight until front measures 11½(11½:11¾:11¾:12¼:12¼)/
29(29:30:30:31:31)cm from cast-on edge, ending with a
wrong side row.

Shape raglan armholes
Next row Bind off 4(5:6:7:8:9) sts, patt to end. *41(43:44:46:48:49) sts.*
Next row Patt to end.
Next row K2, skpo, patt to end.
Next row Patt to end.
Rep the last 2 rows 6(7:8:9:10:11) times more. *34(35:35:36:37:37) sts.*
Change to size 6 (4mm) needles.
Next row K5(6:6:7:8:8), skpo, patt to end.
K 3 rows.
Rep the last 4 rows seven times. *26(27:27:28:29:29) sts.*

Shape front neck
Next row K5(6:6:7:8:8), skpo, k4, turn and leave remaining 15 sts on
a holder.
K 3 rows.
Next row K5(6:6:7:8:8), skpo, k1, skpo.
K 3 rows.
Next row K5(6:6:7:8:8), skpo, k1.
K 3 rows.
Next row K5(6:6:7:8:8), skpo.
K 3 rows. *6(7:7:8:9:9) sts.*
Leave these sts on a spare needle.
Mark position for 7 buttons, the first on the 6th row, the 7th 2 rows below
last row and the remaining 5 spaced evenly between.

RIGHT FRONT
With size 6 (4mm) needles cast on 45(48:50:53:56:58) sts.
Row 1 (WS) K to last 13 sts, p6, k7.
Row 2 K5, p2, k6, p2, k to end.
Row 3 K to last 13 sts, p6, k7.
Row 4 K5, p2, C6F, p2, k to end.
Row 5 K to last 13 sts, p6, k7.
Row 6 (buttonhole row) K2, k2tog, yf, k1, p2, k6, p2, k to end.
Row 7 K to last 13 sts, p6, k7.
Change to size 7 (4.5mm) needles.
Work in patt from Right Front Chart.
Row 1 K5, then p2, k6, p2 from Chart, k to end.
Row 2 P to last 15 sts, k2, p6, k2 from Chart, then k5.
These 2 rows set the 12-row cable panel and g-st front border with
st st body.
Working buttonholes to match markers, cont straight until front measures
11½(11½:11¾:11¾:12¼:12¼)in/29(29:30:30:31:31)cm from cast-on edge,
ending with a right side row.

Shape raglan armhole
Next row Bind off 4(5:6:7:8:9) sts, patt to end. *41(43:44:46:48:49) sts.*
Next row Patt to last 4 sts, k2tog, k2.

Left front

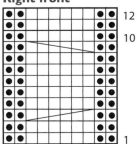

10 sts

Right front

12
10

1

10 sts

KEY
☐ K on RS, P on WS
● P on RS, K on WS
 C6B
 C6F

57

Next row Patt to end.
Rep the last 2 rows 6(7:8:9:10:11) times more. *34(35:35:36:37:37) sts.*
Change to size 6 (4mm) needles.
Next row Patt to last 7(8:8:9:10:10) sts, k2tog, k5(6:6:7:8:8).
K 3 rows.
Rep the last 4 rows 7 times. *26(27:27:28:29:29) sts.*

Shape front neck

Row 1 Decreasing 3 sts over cable, patt 15 sts, leave these 12 sts on a holder, k4, k2tog, k5(6:6:7:8:8).
K 3 rows.
Next row K2tog, k1, k2tog, k5(6:6:7:8:8).
K 3 rows.
Next row K1, k2tog, k5(6:6:7:8:8).
K 3 rows.
Next row K2tog, k5(6:6:7:8:8).
K 3 rows. *6(7:7:8:9:9) sts.*
Leave these sts on a spare needle.

SLEEVES

With size 6 (4mm) needles cast on 38(42:46:50:54:58) sts.
K 7 rows.
Change to size 7 (4.5mm) needles.
Beg with a k row cont in st st.
Work 6 rows.
Inc row K3, m1, k to last 3 sts, m1, k3.
Work 7 rows.
Rep the last 8 rows 10 times and the inc row again. *62(66:70:74:78:82) sts.*
Cont straight until Sleeve measures 17¾in/45cm from cast-on edge, ending with a wrong side row.

Shape raglan sleeve top

Bind off 4(5:6:7:8:9) sts at beg of next 2 rows. *54(56:58:60:62:64) sts.*
Next row K2, skpo, k to last 4 sts, k2 tog, k2.
Next row P to end.
Rep the last 2 rows 6(7:8:9:10:11) times more. *40 sts.*
Change to size 6 (4mm) needles.
Next row K2, skpo, k to last 4 sts, k2 tog, k2.
K 3 rows.
Rep the last 4 rows 11 times. *16 sts*

Left sleeve only

Shape top

Row 1 K2, skpo, k to last 2 sts, wrap 1, turn.
Row 2 K to end.
Row 3 K to last 3 sts, wrap 1, turn.
Row 4 K to end.
Row 5 K2, skpo, k to last 4 sts, wrap 1, turn.
Row 6 K to end.
Row 7 K to last 5 sts, wrap 1, turn.
Row 8 K to end.

Row 9 K2, skpo, k to last 6 sts, wrap 1, turn.
Row 10 K to end.
Row 11 K to last 7 sts, wrap 1, turn.
Row 12 K to end. *13 sts*
Leave these sts on a holder.
Right sleeve only
Shape top
Row 1 K to last 4 sts, k2 tog, k2.
Row 2 K to last 2 sts, wrap 1, turn.
Row 3 K to end.
Row 4 K to last 3 sts, wrap 1, turn.
Row 5 K to last 4 sts, k2 tog, k2.
Row 6 K to last 4 sts, wrap 1, turn.
Row 7 K to end.
Row 8 K to last 5 sts, wrap 1, turn.
Row 9 K to last 4 sts, k2 tog, k2.
Row 10 K to last 6 sts, wrap 1, turn.
Row 11 K to end.
Row 12 K to last 7 sts, wrap 1, turn. *13 sts*
Leave these sts on a holder.

NECKBAND

Join raglan seams.
With right side facing, using size 6 (4mm) needles, place 12 sts from right
front on needle, pick up and k8 sts up right side of front neck, k6(7:7:8:9:9)
sts, k13 sts from right sleeve, 31(32:33:34:35:36) sts from back, 13 sts from
left sleeve, k6(7:7:8:9:9) sts, pick up and k8 sts down left side of front neck,
dec 3 sts over cable, k12 from left front holder.
Next row P10, p2tog, [p2, p2tog] 4 times, p to last 28 sts, p2tog, [p2, p2tog]
four times, p10.
Beg with a k row, work 4 rows in st st.
Bind off.

FINISHING

Join side and sleeve seams. Sew on buttons.

WINDOWPANE PILLOW*

FRONT

Using size 7 (4.5mm) needles cast on 60 sts.

Next row (RS) P1, [k1, p1] 3 times * [knit into front and back of next stitch] twice, [k1, p1] 10 times; rep from * once more, [knit into front and back of next stitch] twice, [k1, p1] 3 times, k1. 66 sts.

Next row K1, [p1, k1] 3 times, p4, *[p1, k1] 10 times, p4; rep from * once more, [p1, k1] 3 times, p1.

Work in patt from Chart.

Row 1 (RS) P1, [k1, p1] 3 times * C4B, [k1, p1] 10 times [ie. the 24-st patt rep]; rep from * once more, C4B, [k1, p1] 3 times, k1.

Row 2 K1, [p1, k1] 3 times p4 * [p1, k1] 10 times, p4 [ie. the 24-st patt rep]; rep from * once more, [p1, k1] 3 times, p1.

SIZE

Pillow measures approx 12in x 12in (30cm x 30cm).

YARN

Pillow 1

3 x 1¾oz/50g balls Hemp Tweed Duck Egg 139. CYCA#4

Pillow 2

3 x 1¾oz/50g balls Rowan Hemp Tweed Misty 137. CYCA#4

NEEDLES

1 pair size 7 (4.5mm) knitting needles.
Cable needle.

GAUGE

19 sts and 32 rows to 4in/10cm square over seed stitch using size 7 (4.5mm) knitting needles.

EXTRAS

12in (30cm) square pillow form.

ABBREVIATIONS

C4B Slip next 2 sts on a cable needle and hold in back of work, k2, then k2 from cable needle.
See also page 127.

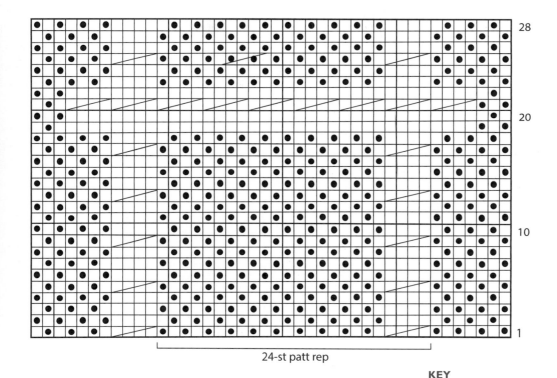

24-st patt rep

KEY

☐ K on RS, P on WS

◉ P on RS, K on WS

▱ C4B

These 2 rows set the Chart and 24-st repeat for the 28-row patt repeat.
Cont in patt to end of row 28.
Rep rows 1 to 28 from Chart twice more, then work rows 1 to 13.
99 rows have been worked in total (WS facing for next row).
Row 100 (WS) K1, [p1, k1] 3 times, [p2tog] twice, *[p1, k1]
10 times, [p2tog] twice; rep from * once more, [p1, k1] 3 times, p1. *60 sts.*
Bind off.

BACK

Using size 7 (4.5mm) needles cast on 59 sts.
Row 1 (RS) K1 * p1, k1; rep from * to end.
Row 2 As Row 1.
These 2 rows form the seed stitch patt.
Repeat these 2 rows until 100 rows have been worked in total with RS
facing for next row.
Bind off.

FINISHING

With RS together, sew front and back along 3 sides. Insert pillow form.
Join rem seam.

SIZE

Blanket measures approx 29½in x 41½in (75cm x 105cm) excluding cable trim.

YARN

Rowan Hemp Tweed 1¾oz/50g balls: CYCA#4
A Almond 141 x 6
B Cameo 140 x 5
C Duck Egg 139 x 1
D Misty 137 x 2
E Treacle 134 x1
F Kelp 142 x 3
G Pumice 138 x 1
H Pine 135 x 1

NEEDLES

1 pair size 7 (4.5mm) knitting needles plus 1 spare size 7 (4.5mm) knitting needle.
Cable needle.

GAUGE

19 sts and 25 rows to 4in/10cm square over st st using size 7 (4.5mm) needles.

62

ABBREVIATIONS

C4B Slip next 2 sts on to a cable needle and hold in back of work, k2 then k2 from cable needle.
C9B Slip next 4 sts on to a cable needle and hold in back of work, k5, then k4 from cable needle.
See also p127.

This throw is made as a patchwork from 35 squares to which the tree and leaf motifs are added, and the squares then joined to make the throw, to which a separate cabled edging is added.

SQUARES

Make 35
Using size 7 (4.5mm) needles and A, cast on 30 sts.
Row 1 (RS) Sl1k, k to end.
Row 2 As Row 1.
Row 3 Sl1k, k to end.
Row 4 Sl1k, k1, P to last 2 sts, k2.
Rep Rows 3 and 4 until 39 rows have been worked in total, with WS facing for next row.
Row 40 (WS) Sl1k, K to end.
Row 41 As row 40.
Next row (WS) Bind off knitwise.
Make a further 17 squares in A (18 in total).
Make 17 squares in B.

TREE MOTIF

Make 17.
Trunk
Using size 7 (US 4.5mm) needles and C, cast on 8 sts.
Row 1 (RS) P2, k4, p2.
Row 2 K2 p4, k2.
Row 3 P2, C4B, p2.
Row 4 As Row 2.
Rep these 4 rows once more, then Rows 1 to 3 inclusive, WS facing for next row.
Row 12 (WS) Ssk, p1, p2tog, p1, k2tog. *5 sts* ***
With RS facing, leave these 5 sts on a spare needle.
Tree
Using size 7 (4.5mm) needles cast on 17 sts with C.
Row 1 (RS) K6, with RS facing place trunk sts on spare needle behind main (left hand) needle and k2tog (the first stitch from main needle and trunk); rep for the next 4 trunk sts; then k6 the remaining sts on main (left hand) needle. Trunk now grafted on.
Row 2 Purl.
Row 3 Ssk, yf, ssk, K to last 4 sts, k2tog, yf, k2tog. *5 sts.*
Row 4 Purl.
Cont to rep Rows 3 and 4, four more times. *7 sts.*
Row 13 (RS) Ssk, yf, sl2K, k1, p2sso, yf, k2tog. *5 sts.*
Row 14 Purl.
Row 15 Ssk, k1, k2tog. *3 sts.*
Row 16 Purl.

Row 17 Sl2k, k1, p2sso. *1 st.*
Fasten off.
Make a further 3 trees in C (4 in total).
Make 4 trees in A.
Make 6 trees in D.
Make 3 trees in E.

LEAF MOTIF

Make 18.
Using size 7 (4.5mm) needles and F cast on 8 sts.
Work trunk as given for Tree Motif to ***. *5sts on needles.*
Cont to work Leaf part as follows:
Row 1 (RS) Knit into front and back of first stitch, k1, yf, k1, yf, k1, k into front and back of last stitch. *9 sts.*
Row 2 Purl.
Row 3 K4, yf, k1, yf, k4. *11 sts.*
Row 4 Purl
Row 5 K5, yf, k1, yf, k5. *13 sts.*
Row 6 Purl.
Row 7 Bind off 3 sts [1 st on right hand needle], k2, yf, k1, yf, k6. *12 sts.*
Row 8 Bind off 3 sts [1 st on right hand needle], p8. *9 sts.*
Rows 9 to 12 As Rows 3 to 6. *13sts.*
Row 13 Bind off 3 sts [1 st on right hand needle], k9. *10 sts*
Row 14 Bind off 3 sts [1 st stitch on right hand needle], p6. *7 sts.*
Row 15 Ssk, k3, k2tog. *5sts.*
Row 16 Purl.
Row 17 Ssk, k1, k2tog. *3 sts.*
Row 18 Purl.
Row 19 Sl1k, k2tog, psso. *1 st.*
Fasten off
Make a further 5 leaves in F [6 in total].
Make 4 leaves in B.
Make 6 leaves in G.
Make 2 leaves in H.

FINISHING

Lightly block, steam and press all squares and motifs; each finished square should measure approx 6in x 6in (15cm x 15cm).
Placing motifs neatly and centrally on each square so that the edges of the trunks run parallel with the rows of knitting, cont as folls:
Sew all Tree motifs to the B yarn squares (the darker-colored squares). Sew all Leaf motifs to the A yarn squares (the lighter-colored squares).
Using a mattress or slip stitch, join all the squares together as shown in the sketch (top right). The squares should form a checkerboard pattern, with a lighter (A yarn) square in each of the four corners.

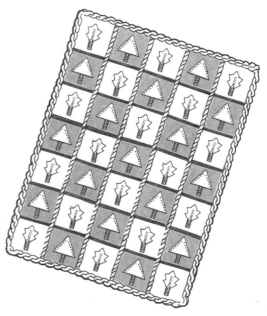

Cable Trim

Using size 7 (4.5mm) needles and F, cast on 11 sts.
Row 1 (RS) P2, k9.
Row 2 P9, k2.
Rows 3 and 4 As Rows 1 and 2.
Row 5 P2, C9B.
Row 6 As Row 2.
Rows 7 to 12 As Rows 1 and 2, three times.
These 12 rows form the patt.
Cont in patt until trim fits around entire edge of joined blanket squares, placing cabled edge at outer edge, and gathering trim at corners so it remains flat, ending with RS facing for next row.
Bind off.
Join ends of trim. Slip stitch trim in place.

63

ARAN KNITS

I created the 13 designs in this section primarily for people who have mastered the basics of cable knitting and are now ready to move into designs with more interesting cable combinations. To this end, I have created simple shaped garments with interesting cable panels as well as items without shaping, such as scarves, pillows and throws.

As the choice of yarn is so important to the way the cable texture looks, I have used Rowan Softyak DK and Rowan Hemp Tweed which show off the more intricate Aran cables very clearly.

The first three patterns in this section are especially chosen as "introductory" designs and patterns for novice Aran knitters, followed by a gallery of further Aran stitch designs and their patterns.

SCARF *

The Aran cable design has a 12-row repeat pattern. It includes two basic cables (C4B and C6B) and a 3-st cable crossing knit and purl stitches (C3R and C3L). It is knitted on a reverse stockinette stitch background with 4 sts of garter stitch at each side to form a border. The pattern is given in chart form showing the 12-row repeat (see page 123 for reading a chart).

SIZE
Approx 8in (20cm) wide x 78¾in (200cm) long.

YARN
6 x 1¾oz/50g balls Rowan Hemp Tweed Pine 135. CYCA#4

NEEDLES
Pair size 7 (4.5mm) needles.
Cable needle.

GAUGE
19 sts and 25 rows to 4in/10cm square over st st using size 7 (4.5mm) needles.

ABBREVIATIONS
C4B Slip next 2 sts on cable needle and hold at back of work, k2, then k2 from cable needle.
C6B Slip next 3 sts on cable needle and hold at back of work, k3, then k3 from cable needle.
C3R Slip next st on cable needle and hold at back of work, k2, then p1 from cable needle.
C3L Slip next 2 sts on cable needle and hold at front of work, p2 , then k2 from cable needle.
sllP ytf Slip one st purlwise with yarn in front of work.
See also page 127.

SCARF
Using US 7 (4.5mm) needles cast on 54 sts.
Rib row 1 (RS) Sllp ytf, k3, p2, * [k2, p2] twice, [k3, p2] twice*; rep from * to * once more, [k2, p2] twice, k4.
Rib row 2 Sllp ytf, k5, * [p2, k2] twice, [p3, k2] twice*; rep from* to * once more, [p2, k2] twice, k4.
Repeat these 2 rows three more times.
Cont to work in patt from Chart.
Chart row 1 (RS) Sllp ytf, k3, p2, k6, * p4, C4B, p4, k6 *, rep from * to *once more, p2, k4.

KEY
☐ RS, K
  WS, P
⊡ RS, P
  WS, K
C3R
C3L
C4B
C6B
▽ sll p ytf on RS and WS

54 sts

66

Chart row 2 Sl1p ytf, k5, p6, * k4, p6, k4, p6 *, rep from * to
*once more, k6.
These 2 rows set the Chart for the 12-row patt rep.
Cont in patt from Chart row 3 to end of Chart row 12.
Now rep rows 1 to 12 from Chart, 39 more times, then Row 1
from Chart once, ending with WS facing for next row.
Next row (WS) Work as Rib row 2.
Now rep Rib rows 1 and 2 three more times, ending with RS
facing for next row.
Bind off in patt.
Scarf completed.

PILLOW *

This pillow has an 8-row repeat pattern. It has 6-st basic cables (C6B and C6F) and a 4-st Aran cable crossing knit over purl stitches (C4R and C4L) knitted on a reversed stockinette stitch background. The rest of the front and all of the back of the pillow are knitted in stockinette stitch. The pattern includes a chart showing the 8-row repeat (see page 123 for reading a chart).

SIZE
15¾in (40cm) square to fit pillow form 16½in (42cm) square.

YARN
4 x 1¾oz/50g balls Rowan Hemp Tweed Duck Egg 139. CYCA#4

NEEDLES
Pair of size 7 (4.5mm) needles.
Cable needle.

EXTRAS
Pillow form 16½in (42cm) square.

GAUGE
19 sts and 25 rows to 4in/10cm square over st st using size 7 (4.5mm) needles.

ABBREVIATIONS
C6B Slip next 3 sts on cable needle and hold at back of work, k3, then k3 from cable needle.
C6F Slip next 3 sts on cable needle and hold at front of work, k3, then k3 from cable needle.
C4R Slip next st on cable needle and hold at back of work, k3, then p1 from cable needle.
C4L Slip next 3 sts on cable needle and hold at front of work, p1, then k3 from cable needle.
See also page 127.

FRONT
Using size 7 (4.5mm) needles cast on 99 sts.
Work in patt from Chart.
Row 1 (RS) K36, work across Row 1 of Chart.
Row 2 Work across Row 2 of Chart, p36.
These 2 rows set the Chart for the 8-row patt repeat with st st to the side.
Cont in patt to end of Chart Row 8.
Now rep rows 1 to 8 from Chart, 11 more times, then Rows 1 to 4 from Chart once, ending with RS facing for next row.
Bind off in patt.

KEY

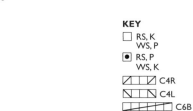

☐ RS, K
　　WS, P
☑ RS, P
　　WS, K
C4R
C4L
C6B
C6F

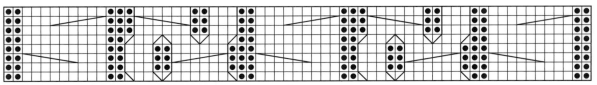

8

63 sts

BACK

Using size 7 (4.5mm) needles cast on 76 sts.
Beg with a k row, work 100 rows in st st.
Bind off.

FINISHING

With WS together, sew back to front along 3 sides using mattress
stitch. Insert the pillow form and join rem seam with mattress stitch.

CAFETIÈRE COZY*

This cafetière cozy has an 8-row repeat pattern. It is knitted on a reverse stockinette stitch background with 4 sts of rib stitch at each end, which form the cafetière side borders. The pattern is given in chart form showing the 8-row repeat (see page 123 for reading a chart).

SIZE
Cozy measures approx 6½in (17cm) x 13in (32.5cm).

YARN
2 x 1¾oz/50g balls Rowan Hemp Tweed Willow 146. CYCA#4

NEEDLES
Pair of size 6 (4mm) and size 7 (4.5mm) needles.
2 cable needles or similar double-pointed needles.

EXTRAS
3 large buttons.

GAUGE
19 sts and 25 rows to 4in (10cm) square over st st using size 7 (4.5mm) needles.

ABBREVIATIONS
C4B Slip next 2 sts on cable needle and hold at back of work, k2, then k2 from cable needle.
C4F Slip next 2 sts on cable needle and hold at front of work, k2, then k2 from cable needle.
C6B Slip next 3 sts on cable needle and hold at back of work, k3, then k3 from cable needle.
C6F Slip next 3 sts on cable needle and hold at front of work, k3, then k3 from cable needle.
C5R Slip next 2 sts onto cable needle and hold at back of work, k3, then p2 from cable needle.
C5L Slip next 3 sts on cable needle and hold at front of work, p2, then k3 from cable needle.
See also page 127.

CAFETIÈRE COZY (to fit classic 8-cup cafetière)
Using size 6 (4mm) needles cast on 59 sts.
Rib row 1 (RS) K2, p1, k1, p2, k4, p3, [k3, p3] 6 times, k4, p2, k1, p1, k2.
Rib row 2 [K1, p1] twice, k2, p4, k3, [p3, k3] 6 times, p4, k2, [p1, k1] twice.
Repeat these 2 rows, 3 more times, ending with RS facing for next row.
Change to size 7 (4.5mm) needles and work from Chart.
Chart row 1 (RS) K2, p1, k1, p2, k4, p2, k3, p4, [C6F, p4] 3 times, k4, p2, k1, p1, k2.

70

KEY
☐ RS, K
WS, P
⊡ RS, P
WS, K
▱ C5R
▱ C5L
▱ C4B
▱ C4F
▱ C6B
▱ C6F

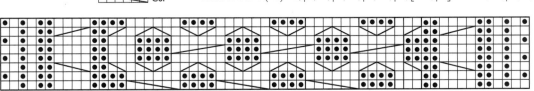

59 sts

Chart row 2 [K1, p1] twice, k2, p4, k4, [p6, k4] 3 times, p3, k2, p4, k2, [p1, k1] twice.

These 2 rows set the Chart for the 8-row patt repeat.

Cont in patt from Chart row 3 to end of Chart row 8.

Now rep Rows 1 to 8 from Chart, 7 more times, then Rows 1 to 5 from Chart once, ending with WS facing for next row.

Change to size 6 (4mm) needles.

Next row (WS) Work as Rib row 2.

Now rep Rib rows 1 and 2 three times. Bind off in patt.

FINISHING
Cord button-loops (make 3)

Using two cable needles or similar double-pointed needles, cast on 3 sts.

Row 1 (RS) K3, * without turning work,

slip these 3 sts to opposite end of needle and bring yarn to opposite end of work, pulling it quite tightly across the back of these 3 sts. Using other needle, k these 3 sts again. Rep from * until cord is approx. 3in (7.5mm) long. Bind off.

Make two more cords in the same way. Mark position of first loop on cozy at midway point of rib and of the other two loops at 1in (2.5mm) from side edge of cozy. Fold each cord in half to form a loop and sew securely approx 1in (2.5mm) from the ends of each loop along one **WS** rib edge of cozy, leaving approx. ¾ to 1in (2 to 2.5mm) of loop showing. Attach buttons to RS opposite rib edge of cozy, aligning button edge with cast-on/bound-off edge.

LONG ARAN SCARF

This simple, extra long scarf is an easy-to-knit Aran design, with a honeycomb central cable panel and plaited cable borders. Knitted in Rowan Softyak DK yarn. *Pattern on page 114.*

DEEP ARAN COWL

This extra deep, slightly shaped cowl has a repeating Aran pattern with a ribbed top and bottom. Knitted in Rowan Softyak DK yarn. *Pattern on page 110.*

ARAN HAT FOR HIM/HER

This longer-than-usual Aran bobble hat comes in two sizes. It is knitted in Rowan Softyak DK yarn. *Pattern on page 108.*

LONG ARAN CARDIGAN

This elegant edge-to-edge Aran cardigan has a garter-stitch buttonband and ribbed hem and cuffs. The rope-twist cable pattern is on the fronts only. It is knitted in Rowan Softyak DK yarn. *Pattern on page 98.*

ARAN WRAP

The Aran pattern on this wrap is quite complicated but the wrap requires no
shaping. It is long enough to be worn over one shoulder, and is knitted in
Rowan Softyak DK yarn. *Pattern on page 120.*

CLASSIC ARAN SWEATER

Everyone wants a really good classic Aran sweater pattern and this simplified one
has an Aran panel on the front and back. It makes a great knit for him or her: in
the photographs, Martin and his niece, Harriet, are wearing the same size
sweater. It is knitted in Rowan Hemp Tweed. *Pattern on page 94.*

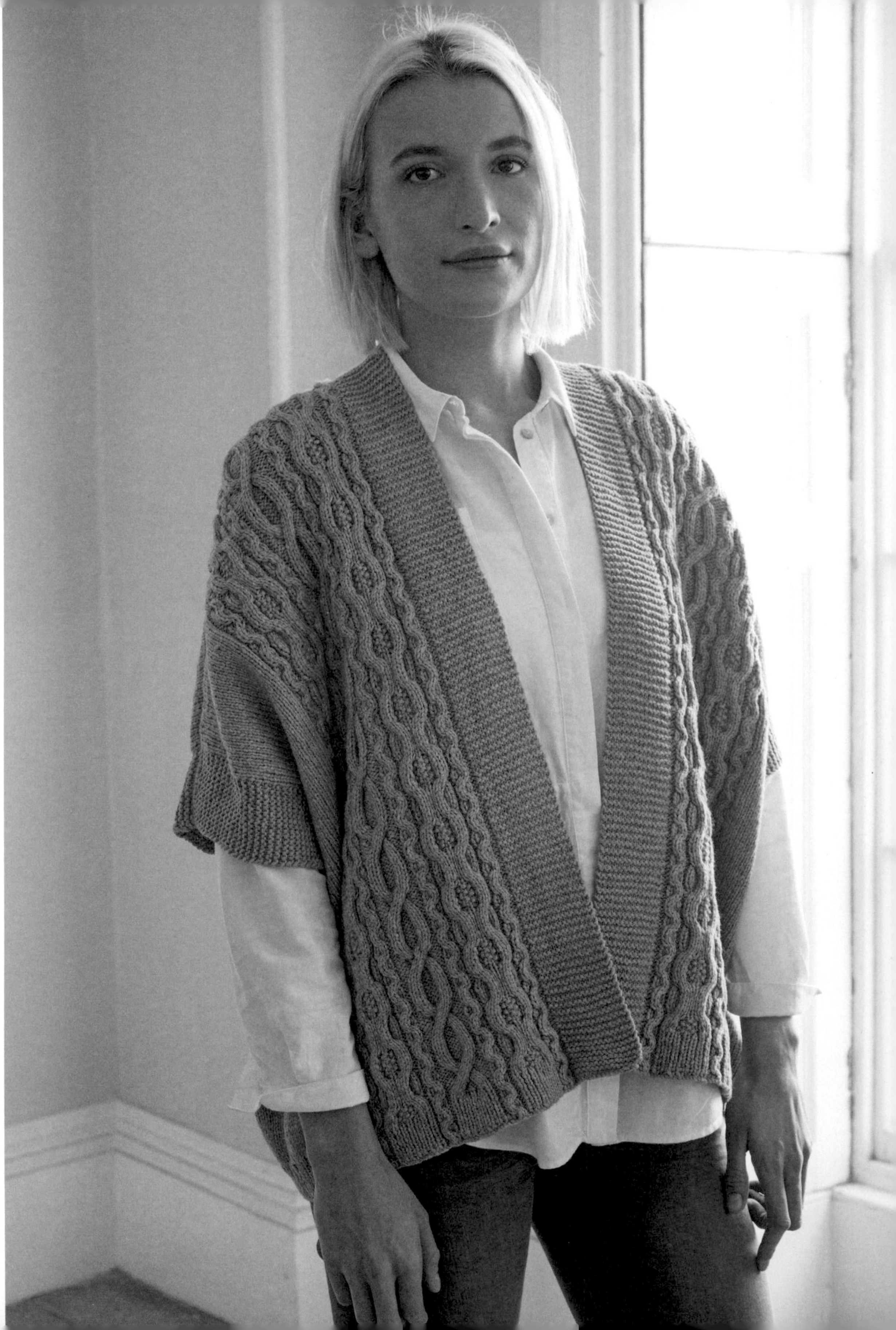

ARAN PONCHO JACKET

This is a great jacket design, as it has very simple shaping.
The edge-to-edge fronts have an attractive Aran pattern. It is knitted
in Rowan Softyak DK yarn. *Pattern on page 102.*

SQUARE ARAN PILLOW

Another good first-time Aran knit, with an Aran design on part
of the pillow front only, knitted in Rowan Softyak DK yarn.

Pattern on page 106.

ARAN THROW

This great throw features three different cable patterns making up a glorious
Aran design for a sofa or an end-of-bed, or simply to wrap yourself in. It is knitted
in Rowan Softyak DK yarn. *Pattern on page 116.*

RECTANGULAR ARAN PILLOW

This elegant rectangular pillow features a central Aran panel on a
stockinette stitch background. A good first-time Aran project, it is knitted
in Rowan Softyak DK yarn. *Pattern on page 112.*

ARAN PATTERNS

When knitting an Aran cable pattern, you must take care to look at the abbreviations **very** carefully before you start, to make sure you understand exactly what you are doing. Each pattern carries its own special abbreviations, but there is also a list of general abbreviations used in the book on page 127.

The fitted garments give a range of sizes and their actual measurements (including ease) for the bust sizes given.

The patterns are given star ratings, so those marked * are the best ones to work on first, as they are small projects with no shaping, while the Aran garments that are shaped to fit are marked ***. When knitting garments, it is essential to work to the gauge provided (and to change the needles to a size larger or smaller if your gauge is respectively too tight or too loose). See notes on pages 122-127 for further information on working to gauge and on the * ratings used in this book.

CLASSIC ARAN SWEATER ***

To fit bust/chest

32-34	36-38	40-42	44-46	in
81-86	91-97	102-107	112-117	cm

Actual measurements

Bust/Chest

37	42	46½	51½	in
94	107	118	131	cm

Length to shoulder

26¾	27½	28¼	29	in
68	70	72	74	cm

BACK

With size 6 (4mm) needles cast on 99(111:123:135) sts.
Rib row 1 (RS) K3, [p2, k2] to end.
Rib row 2 P3, [k2, p2] to end.
Rep the last 2 rows 9 times more, inc one st at center of last row.
100(112:124:136) sts.
Change to size 7 (4.5mm) needles.
Row 1 K19(25:31:37), work across Row 1 of Chart, k19(25:31:37).
Row 2 P19(25:31:37), work across Row 2 of Chart, p19(25:31:37).
These 2 rows set the position for the 24-row cable panel and forms the st st to sides.
Cont to work in patt until back measures 15¼(15¾:16:16½)in/39(40:41:42)cm from cast-on edge, ending with a wrong side row.
Shape raglan armholes
Bind off 6(8:10:12) sts at beg of next 2 rows. *88(96:104:112) sts.*
Patt 4 rows.
Next row K2, skpo, patt to last 4 sts, k2tog, k2.
Next row Patt to end.
Rep the last 6 rows 3(2:1:0) times. *80(90:100:110) sts.* **
Patt 2 rows.
Next row K2, skpo, patt to last 4 sts, k2tog, k2.
Next row Patt to end.
Rep the last 4 rows 7(9:11:13) times. *64(70:76:82) sts.*
Bind off in patt.

FRONT

Work as given for Back to **.
Patt 2 rows.
Next row K2, skpo, patt to last 4 sts, k2tog, k2.
Next row Patt to end.
Rep the last 4 rows 4(6:8:10) times. *70(76:82:88) sts.*
Shape front neck
Next row Patt 24(26:28:30), work2tog, turn and work on these sts for first side of neck shaping.

YARN
13(14:15:16) x 1¾oz/50g balls
Rowan Hemp Tweed
Almond 141. CYCA#4

94

NEEDLES
Pair each size 6 (4mm) and size 7 (4.5mm) knitting needles.
Cable needle.

GAUGE
19 sts and 25 rows to 4in/10cm square over st st using size 7 (4.5mm) needles.
Cable panel (62sts) measures 11in (28cm) across width.

Next row Patt to end.
Next row K2, skpo, patt to last 2 sts, skpo.
Next row Patt to end.
Next row Patt to last 2 sts, skpo.
Rep the last 4 rows once and the first 3 rows again. *17(19:21:23) sts.*
Bind off in patt.
With right side facing, place center 18(20:22:24) sts on a holder, rejoin yarn to rem sts, work 2tog, patt to end.
Next row Patt to end.
Next row K2tog, patt to last 4 sts, k2tog, k2.
Next row Patt to end.
Next row K2tog, patt to end.
Rep the last 4 rows once and the first 3 rows again. *17(19:21:23) sts.*
Bind off in patt.

SLEEVES
With size 6 (4mm) needles cast on 39(43:47:51) sts.
Rib row 1 K3, [p2, k2] to end.
Rib row 2 P3, [k2, p2] to end.
These 2 rows form the rib.
Rep last 2 rows 9 times, inc 0(2:4:6) sts evenly across last row. *39(45:51:57) sts.*

ABBREVIATIONS
T5B Slip next 3 sts on a cable needle and hold at back of work, k2, slip center st back onto left hand needle, p this st, then k2 from cable needle.
C7B Slip next 4 sts on a cable needle and hold at back of work, k3, then k4 from cable needle.
C3R Slip next st on a cable needle and hold at back of work, k2, then p1 from cable needle.
C3L Slip next 2 sts on a cable needle and hold at front of work, p1, then k2 from cable needle.
C4R Slip next st on a cable needle and hold at back of work, k3, then p1 from cable needle.
C4L Slip next 3 sts on a cable needle and hold at front of work, p1, then k3 from cable needle.
C4R-K Slip next st on a cable needle and hold at back of work, k3, then k1 from cable needle.
C4L-K Slip next 3 sts on a cable needle and leave at front of work, k1, then k3 from cable needle.
See also page 127.

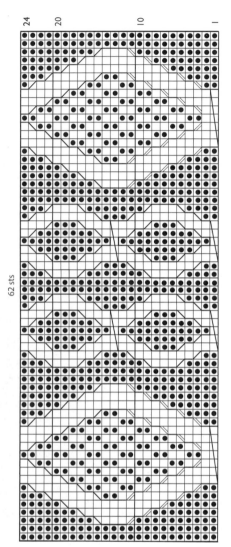

Change to size 7 (4.5mm) needles.

Beg with a k row work in st st.

Work 6 rows.

Inc row 1 K4, M1, k to last 4 sts, M1, k4.

Work 5 rows.

Rep the last 6 rows 15 times and the first inc row again. *73(79:85:91) sts.*

Cont straight until sleeve measures 20in/51cm from cast-on edge, ending with a wrong side row.

Shape raglan top

Bind off 6(8:10:12) sts at beg of next 2 rows. *61(63:65:67) sts.*

Work 2 rows.

Next row K2, skpo, k to last 4 sts, k2tog, k2.

Next row P to end.

Rep the last 4 rows 9 times. *41(43:45:47) sts.* **

Next row K2, skpo, to last 4 sts, k2tog, k2.

Next row P to end.

Rep the last 2 rows 7(8:9:10) times. *25 sts.*

Left sleeve only

Work 22(24:28:30) rows straight, ending with a p row.

Next row K12, turn, leave remaining 13 sts for front saddle on a holder, work on these 12 sts for a further 13(15:15:17) rows for back saddle.
Bind off.

Right sleeve only

Work 21(23:27:31) rows straight, ending with a k row.

Next row P12, turn, leave remaining 13 sts for front saddle on a holder, work on these 12 sts for a further 14(16:16:18) rows for back saddle.
Bind off.

NECKBAND

Join both front saddle and armhole seams.

With right side facing, using size 6 (4.5mm) needles, pick up and k14(15:16:17) sts along row ends of left sleeve extension, k across 12 sts from left sleeve holder, pick up and k9 sts down left side of front neck, k18(20:22:24) sts across center front holder, pick up and k8 sts up right side of front neck, k across 12 sts from right sleeve holder, pick up and k14(15:16:17) sts along row ends of right sleeve extension. *87(91:95:99) sts.*

Rib row 1 (WS) K3, [p2, k2] to end.

Rib row 2 P3, [k2, p2] to end.

These 2 rows form the rib.

Work a further 11 rows.

Bind off in rib.

FINISHING

Join bound-off edges of back sleeve extensions and neckband. Join back shoulder saddle and armhole seams. Join side and sleeve seams.

KEY

- ☐ RS, K / WS, P
- ● RS, P / WS, K
- C3R
- C3L
- C4R
- C4L
- C4R-K
- C4L-K
- T5B
- C7B

LONG ARAN CARDIGAN***

To fit bust

32-34	36-38	40-42	44-46	in
81-86	91-97	102-107	112-117	cm

Actual measurements

Bust

40	44½	49	53	in
102	113	124	135	cm

Length to back neck

32¾	33½	34¼	35	in
83	85	87	89	cm

Sleeve length 17¾in/45cm

BACK

Using size 5 (3.75mm) needles, cast on 126(138:150:162) sts.

1st and 3rd sizes only

Rib row 1 (RS) P2, [k2, p2] to end.

Rib row 2 K2, [p2, k2] to end.

2nd and 4th sizes only

Rib row 1 (RS) K2, [p2, k2] to end.

Rib row 2 P2, [k2, p2] to end.

All sizes

These 2 rows form the rib.

Work a further 8 rows.

Change to size 6 (4mm) needles.

Beg with a k row, cont in st st.

Work 24 rows.

Dec row K4, skpo, k to last 6 sts, k2tog, k4.

Work 23 rows.

Rep last 24 rows 4 times more and the dec row again. *114(126:138:150) sts.*

Cont in st st until back measures 24¾(25¼:25¾:26)in/63(64:65:66)cm from cast-on edge, ending with a wrong side row.

Mark each end of last row with a colored thread.

Cont in st st until back measures 31½(32¼:33:34)in/80(82:84:86)cm from cast-on edge, ending with a wrong side row.

Shape upper arms

Bind off 6(7:8:9) sts at beg of next 6 rows and 7 sts at beg of foll 2 rows. 64(70:76:82) sts.

Shape shoulders

Bind off 8(9:10:11) sts at beg of next 4 rows.

Bind off rem 32(34:36:38) sts.

LEFT FRONT

Using size 5 (3.75mm) needles, cast on 63(69:75:81) sts.

Rib row 1 (RS) K0(2:0:2), [p2, k2] 2(3:5:6) times, p3, k3, p2, [k2, p2] twice, k3, p3, k4, p3, k3, p2, [k2, p2] twice, k3, p3, k6, sl1p ytf.

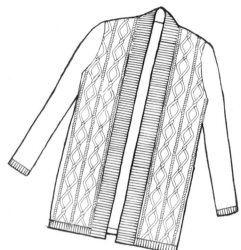
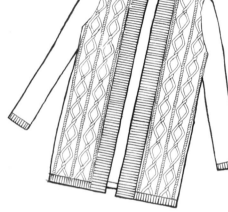

YARN

11(12:14:15) x 1¾/50g balls of Rowan Softyak DK Plain 232. CYCA#3

NEEDLES

Pair each of size 5 (3.75mm) and size 6 (4mm) knitting needles. Cable needle.

GAUGE

22 sts and 30 rows to 4in/10cm over st st using size 6 (4mm). needles.

Rib row 2 K10, p3, k2, [p2, k2] twice, p3, k3, p4, k3, p3, k2, [p2, k2] twice, p3, k3, [p2, k2] 2(3:5:6) times, p0(2:0:2).

Rib row 3 K0(2:0:2), [p2, k2] 2(3:5:6) times, p3, k3, p2, [k2, p2] twice, k3, p3, C4B, p3, k3, p2, [k2, p2] twice, k3, p3, k6, sl1p ytf.

Rib row 4 K10, p3, k2, [p2, k2] twice, p3, k3, p4, k3, p3, k2, [p2, k2] twice, p3, k3, [p2, k2] 2(3:5:6) times, p0(2:0:2).

These 4 rows form the rib.

Work a further 5 rows.

Inc row K10, p3, k2, [p1, M1p, p1, k2] twice, p3, k3, p4, k3, p3, k2, [p1, M1p, p1, k2] twice, p3, k3, [p2, k2] 2(3:5:6) times, p0(2:0:2). *67(73:79:85) sts.*

Change to size 6 (4mm) needles.

Row 1 (RS) K8(14:20:26), work across Row 1 of Chart, k6, sl1p ytf.

Row 2 K7, work across Row 2 of Chart, p8(14:20:26).

These 2 rows set the Chart with st st to the side.

Patt a further 22 rows.

Dec row K1(3:5:7), skpo, patt to end.

Patt 23 rows.

Rep the last 24 rows 4 times more and the dec row again. *61(67:73:79) sts.*

Cont in patt until left front measures 24¾(25¼:25¾:26)in/63(64:65:66)cm from cast-on edge, ending with a wrong side row.

Mark end of last row with a colored thread.

Cont in patt until left front measures 31½(32¼:33:34)in/80(82:84:86)cm from cast-on edge, ending with a wrong side row.

ABBREVIATIONS

C4B Slip next 2 sts on cable needle and hold at back of work, k2 then k2 from cable needle.

C6B Slip next 3 sts on cable needle and hold at back of work, k3, then k3 from cable needle.

C4R Slip next st on cable needle and hold at back of work, k3, then p1 from cable needle.

C4L Slip next 3 sts on cable needle and hold at front of work, p1, then k3 from cable needle.

See also page 127.

Shape upper arm
Bind off 8(9:10:11) sts at beg of next and 2 foll right side rows.
Work 1 row.
Bind off 9(10:11;12)sts at beg of foll row. *28(30:32:34) sts.*
Work 1 row.

Shape shoulder
Bind off 10(11:12:13) sts at beg of next and foll right side row. *8 sts.*
Cont in g-st with slip st edging until border fits halfway across back neck.
Bind off.

RIGHT FRONT
Using size 5 (3.75mm) needles, cast on 63(69:75:81) sts.
Rib row 1 (RS) Sl1p ytf, k6, p3, k3, p2, [k2, p2] twice, k3, p3, k4, p3, k3, p2, [k2, p2] twice, k3, p3, [k2, p2] 2(3:5:6) times, k0(2:0:2).
Rib row 2 P0(2:0:2), [k2, p2] 2(3:5:6) times, k3, p3, k2, [p2, k2] twice, p3, k3, p4, k3, p3, k2, [p2, k2] twice, p3, k10.
Rib row 3 Sl1p ytf, k6, p3, k3, p2, [k2, p2] twice, k3, p3, C4B, p3, k3, p2, [k2, p2] twice, k3, p3, [k2, p2] 2(3:56) times, k0(2:0:2).
Rib row 4 P0(2:0:2), [k2, p2] 2(3:5:6) times, k3, p3, k2, [p2, k2] twice, p3, k3, p4, k3, p3, k2, [p2, k2] twice, p3, k10.
These 4 rows form the rib.
Work a further 5 rows.
Inc row P0(2:0:2), [k2, p2] 2(3:5:6) times, k3, p3, k2, [p1, M1p, p1, k2] twice, p3, k3, p4, k3, p3, k2, [p1, M1p, p1, k2] twice, p3, k10. *67(73:79:85) sts.*
Change to size 6 (4mm) needles.
Row 1 Sl1p ytf, k6, work across Row 1 of Chart, k8(14:20:26).
Row 2 P8(14:20:26), work across Row 2 of Chart, k7.
These 2 rows set the Chart with st st to the side.
Patt a further 22 rows.
Dec row Patt to last 3(5:7:9) sts, k2tog, k1(3:5:7).
Patt 23 rows.
Rep the last 24 rows 4 times more and the dec row again. *61(67:73:79 sts.*
Cont in patt until right front measures 24¾(25¼:25¾:26)in/63(64:65:66)cm from cast-on edge, ending with a wrong side row.
Mark beg of last row with a colored thread.
Cont in patt until right front measures 31½(32¼:33:34)in/80(82:84:86)cm from cast-on edge, ending with a right side row.

Shape upper arm
Bind off 8(9:10:11) sts at beg of next and 2 foll wrong side rows.
Work 1 row.
Bind off 9(10:11:12)sts at beg of foll row. *28(30:32:34) sts.*
Work 1 row.

Shape shoulder

Bind off 10(11:12:13) sts at beg of next and foll wrong side row. *8 sts.*
Cont in g-st with slip st edging until border fits halfway across back neck.
Bind off.

SLEEVES

Using size 5 (3.75mm) needles, cast on 50(54:58:62) sts.
Rib row 1 (RS) K2, [p2, k2] to end.
Rib row 2 P2, [k2, p2] to end.
These 2 rows form the rib.
Work a further 18 rows.
Change to size 6 (4mm) needles.
Beg with a k row cont in st st.
Work 6 rows.
Inc row K5, m1, k to last 5 sts, M1, k5.
Work 7 rows.
Rep the last 8 rows 11 times more and the Inc row again. *76(80:84:88) sts.*
Work straight until sleeve measures 17¾in/45cm from cast-on edge, ending
with a wrong side row.
Shape top
Bind off 4 sts at beg of next 16 rows.
Bind off rem 12(16:20:24) sts.

FINISHING

Join bound-off edges of border. Sew row ends to back neck. With center of
sleeve head to upper arm seam, sew in sleeves between markers. Join side
and sleeve seams.

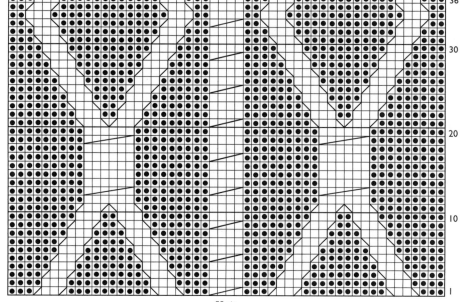

KEY
- ☐ RS, K / WS, P
- ☑ RS, P / WS, K
- C4R
- C4L
- C4B
- C6B

52 sts

YARN

11(12:13:15) x 1¾/50g balls Rowan Softyak DK Steppe 231. CYCA#3

102

NEEDLES

Pair each size 3 (3.25mm) and size 6 (4mm) knitting needles.
Circular size 3 (3.25mm) and size 6 (4mm) knitting needles.
Cable needle.

GAUGE

22 sts and 30 rows to 4in/10cm square over st st using size 6 (4mm) needles.

ARAN PONCHO JACKET**

To fit bust

36-38	40-42	44-46	48-50	in
91-97	102-107	112-117	122-127	cm

Finished measurements

Bust

50	55	60	66	in
127	140	152	165	cm

Length to back neck

26¾	27½	28¼	29	in
68	70	72	74	cm

BACK

With size 3 (3.25mm) circular needle cast on 141(155:169:183) sts.
Work backwards and forwards in rows.

1st and 3rd sizes only

Rib row 1 (RS) P1, [k1, p1] to end.
Rib row 2 K1, [p1, k1] to end.

2nd and 4th sizes only

Rib row 1 (RS) K1, [p1, k1] to end.
Rib row 2 P1, [k1, p1] to end.
These 2 rows form the rib.
Work a further 10 rows.
Change to size 6 (4mm) circular needle.
Beg with a k row, work in st st until back measures 13¾(14¼:14½:15) in/35(36:37:38)cm from cast-on edge, ending with a wrong side row.

Armhole borders

Row 1 Cast on 15 sts, k to end.

Row 2 Cast on 15 sts, k these 15 sts, p to last 15 sts, k15. *171(185:199:213) sts.*

Row 3 K to end.

Row 4 K15, p to last 15 sts, k15.

Last 2 rows form the st st with g-st edging.

Cont in patt until back measures 23(23½:24½:25¼)in/58(60:62:64)cm from cast-on edge, ending with a wrong side row.

Shape upper arms and shoulders

Bind off 15 sts at beg of next 2 rows. *141(155:169:183) sts*

Bind off 6 sts at beg of next 2 rows. *129(143:157:171) sts.*

Bind off 4(5:5:6) sts at beg of the next 2 rows.

Bind off 5(5:6:6) sts at beg of next 2 rows.

Rep the last 4 rows 6 times more. *3 sts.*

Next row Work 3tog and fasten off.

LEFT FRONT

With size 3 (3.25mm) needles cast on 110(117:124:131) sts.

Row 1 K0(1:0:1), [p1, k1] 12(15:19:22) times, * p2, k4, p2, [k1, p1] 6 times, k1 *, rep from * to * twice more, p2, k4, p2, k15.

Row 2 K15, k2, p4, k2, * p1, [k1, p1] 6 times, k2, p4, k2 *, rep from * to * twice more, [p1,k1] 12(15:19:22) times, p0(1:0:1).

Row 3 K0(1:0:1), [p1, k1] 12(15:19:22) times, * p2, C4F, p2, [k1, p1] 6 times, k1 *, rep from * to * twice more, p2, C4F, p2, k15.

Row 4 As row 2.

Rows 5 and 6 As rows 1 and 2.

Row 7 K0(1:0:1), [p1, k1] 12(15:19:22) times, * p2, C4B, p2, [k1, p1] 6 times, k1 *, rep from * to * twice more, p2, C4B, p2, k15.

Row 8 As row 2.

Rep rows 1 to 4, once more.

ABBREVIATIONS

C4B Slip next 2 sts on a cable needle, hold at back of work, k2, then k2 from cable needle.

C4F Slip next 2 sts on a cable needle, hold at front of work, k2, then k2 from cable needle.

C6B Slip next 3 sts on a cable needle, hold at back of work, k3, then k3 from cable needle.

C6F Slip next 3 sts on a cable needle, hold at front of work, k3, then k3 from cable needle.

T7B Slip next 4 sts on a cable needle, hold at back of work, k3, then slip center st back onto left hand needle, p this st, then k3 from cable needle.

C4R Slip next st on a cable needle, hold at back of work, k3, then p1 from cable needle.

C4L Slip next 3 sts on a cable needle, hold at front of work, p1, then k3 from cable needle.

C5R Slip next 2 sts on a cable needle, hold at back of work, k3, then p2 from cable needle.

C5L Slip next 3 sts on a cable needle, hold at front of work, p2, then k3 from cable needle.

See also page 127.

KEY

□	RS, K / WS, P	
▣	RS, P / WS, K	
	C4B	C4L
	C4F	C5R
	C4R	C5L
		C6B
		C6F
		T7B

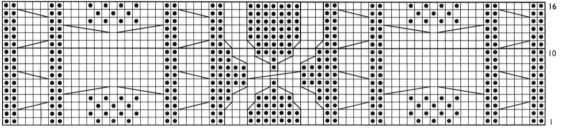

71 sts

Change to size 6 (4mm) needles.

Work in patt from Chart.

Row 1 K24(31:38:45), work across Row 1 of Chart, k15.

Row 2 K15, work across Row 2 of Chart, p24(31:38:45).

These 2 rows set the 16-row patt rep with g-st front border and st st to side.

Cont in patt until front measures 13¾(14¼:14½:15)in/35(36:37:38)cm from cast-on edge, ending with a wrong side row.

Armhole border

Row 1 Cast on 15 sts, k these 15 sts, then patt to end.

Row 2 Patt to last 15 sts, k15. *125(132:139:146) sts.*

Row 3 K15, patt to end.

Row 4 Patt to last 15 sts, k15.

Last 2 rows continue the cable panel with g-st armhole border.

Cont in patt until left front measures 23(23½:24½:25¼)in/58(60:62:64)cm from cast-on edge, ending with a wrong side row.

Shape shoulder

Next row Bind off 15 sts, patt to end. *110(117:124:131) sts.*

Work 1 row.

Next row Bind off 6 sts, patt to end. *104(111:118:125) sts.*

Work 1 row.

Next row Bind off 4(5:5:6) sts, patt to end.

Work 1 row.

Next row Bind off 5(5:6:6) sts, patt to end.

Work 1 row.

Rep the last 4 rows once. *86(91:96:101) sts.*

Next row Bind off 7(7:8:8) sts, patt to end.

Work 1 row.

Next row Bind off 7(8:8:9) sts, patt to end.

Work 1 row.

Rep the last 4 rows 4 times more. *16 sts.*

Bind off.

RIGHT FRONT

With size 3 (3.25mm) needles cast on 110(117:124:131) sts.

Row 1 K15, * p2, k4, p2, [k1, p1] 6 times, k1 *, rep from * to * twice more, p2, k4, p2, [k1, p1] 12(15:19:22) times, k0(1:0:1).

Row 2 P0(1:0:1), [k1, p1] 12(15:19:22) times, k2, p4, k2, * p1, [k1, p1] 6 times, k2, p4, k2 *, rep from * to * twice more, k15.

Row 3 K15, * p2, C4F, p2, [k1, p1] 6 times, k1 *, rep from * to * twice more, p2, C4F, p2, [k1, p1] 12(15:19:22) times, k0(1:0:1).

Row 4 As row 2.

Rows 5 and 6 As rows 1 and 2.

Row 7 K15, * p2, C4B, p2, [k1, p1] 6 times, k1 *, rep from * to * twice more, p2, C4B, p2, [k1, p1] 12(15:19:22) times, k0(1:0:1).

Row 8 As row 2.

Rep rows 1 to 4, once more.

Change to size 6 (4mm) needles.

Work in patt from Chart.

Row 1 K15, work across Row 1 of Chart, k24(31:38:45).

Row 2 P24(31:38:45), work across Row 2 of Chart, k15.

These last 2 rows set the 16-row patt rep with g-st front border and st st to side.

Cont in patt until right front measures 13¾(14¼:14½:15)in/35(36:37:38)cm from cast-on edge, ending with a right side row.

Armhole border

Row 1 (WS) Cast on 15 sts, k these 15 sts, then patt to end.

Row 2 Patt to last 15 sts, k15. *125(132:139:146) sts.*

Row 3 K15, patt to end.

Row 4 Patt to last 15 sts, k15.

Last 2 rows continue the cable panel with g-st border for armhole border.

Cont in patt until right front measures 23(23½:24½:25¼)in/58(60:62:64)cm from cast-on edge, ending with a right side row.

Shape shoulder

Next row Bind off 15 sts, patt to end. *110(117:124:131) sts.*

Work 1 row.

Next row Bind off 6 sts, patt to end. *104(111:118:125) sts.*

Work 1 row.

Next row Bind off 4(5:5:6) sts, patt to end.

Work 1 row.

Next row Bind off 5(5:6:6) sts, patt to end.

Work 1 row.

Rep the last 4 rows once. *86(91:96:101) sts.*

Next row Bind off 7(7:8:8) sts. patt t end.

Work 1 row

Next row Bind off 7(8:8:9) sts, patt to end.

Work 1 row.

Rep the last 4 rows 4 times more. *16 sts.*

Bind off.

FINISHING

Join shoulder seams. Join bound-off edges of front bands. Join side and cast-on edges of armbands.

SQUARE ARAN PILLOW**

BACK
Using size 5 (3.75mm) needles cast on 86 sts.
Beg with a k row, work 114 rows in st st.
Bind off.

FRONT
Using size 5 (3.75mm) needles cast on 86 sts.
K 1 row.
Inc row P4, [M1, p2] 19 times, M1, p44. *106 sts.*
Work in patt.
Row 1 (RS) K36, work across Row 1 of Chart, p1.
Row 2 K1, work across Row 2 of Chart, p36.
These 2 rows set the Chart with st st to the side.
Cont in patt to end of Row 26.
Repeat rows 3 to 26 for a further 84 rows, ending with a RS row.
Dec row K43, [k2tog, k1] 19 times, k2tog, k4. *86 sts.*
P 1 row.
Bind off.

FINISHING
With right sides together, sew the back to the front along 3 sides. Insert the pillow form and join the remaining seam.

SIZE
15in (38cm) square to fit a pillow form 15¾in (40cm) square.

YARN
3 x 1¾oz/50g balls of Rowan Softyak DK Plain 232. CYCA#3

NEEDLES
Pair size 5 (3.75mm) knitting needles.
Cable needle.

EXTRAS
Pillow form 15¾in (40cm) square.

GAUGE
23 sts and 33 rows to 4in/10cm square over st st using size 5 (3.75mm) needles.

ABBREVIATIONS

C4B Slip next 2 sts on cable needle, hold at back of work, k2, then k2 from cable needle.

C4F Slip next 2 sts on cable needle, hold at front of work, k2, then k2 from cable needle.

C6B Slip next 3 sts on cable needle, hold at back of work, k3, then k3 from cable needle.

C6F Slip next 3 sts on cable needle, hold at front of work, k3, then k3 from cable needle.

C5R Slip next 2 sts on cable needle, hold at back of work, k3, then p2 from cable needle.

C5L Slip next 3 sts on cable needle, hold at front of work, p2, then k3 from cable needle.

Make bobble [K1, yf, k1, yf, k1] all into next st, turn, p5, turn, k5, turn and p2tog, p1, p2tog, turn and sl 1, k2tog, psso to complete bobble.

See also page 127.

KEY

□ RS, K WS, P	▨ ▨ C5R
⊡ RS, P WS, K	▨ ▨ C5L
▨▨ C4B	▨▨▨ C6B
▨▨ C4F	▨▨▨ C6F
	■ Make Bobble

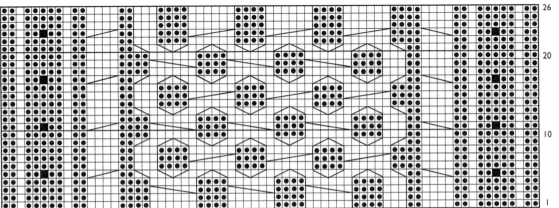

69 sts

SIZE

To fit average woman's (man's) head.

YARN

3 x 1¾oz/50g balls of Rowan Softyak DK in Steppe 231 or Lawn 241. CYCA#3

NEEDLES

Pair each size 3 (3.25mm) and size 6 (4mm) knitting needles. Cable needle.

GAUGE

22 sts and 30 rows to 4in/10cm square over st st using size 6 (4mm) needles.
32 sts and 30 rows to 4in/10cm square over cable patt using using size 6 (4mm) needles.

TO MAKE

Her Version

Using size 3 (3.25mm) needles cast on 167 sts.

Rib row 1 (RS) P2, * k4, [p2, k3] twice, p2, k4, p2, k3, p3, k3, p2 *, rep from * to * 4 times more.

Rib row 2 * K2, p3, k3, p3, k2, p4, k2, [p3, k2] twice, p4 *, rep from * to * 4 times more, k2.

Rib row 3 P2, * C4B, [p2, k3] twice, p2, C4B, p2, k3, p3, k3, p2 *, rep from * to * 4 times more.

Rib row 4 As row 2.

These 4 rows set the patt.

Work a further 8 rows.

Change to size 6 (4mm) needles and cont in patt from Chart.

Row 1 P2, [work across Row 1 of 33-st patt rep of Chart] 5 times.

Row 2 [Work across Row 2 of 33-st patt rep of Chart] 5 times, k2.

These 2 rows set Chart for the 24-row rep and rev st st.

Cont in patt from Chart Row 3 to end of Chart row 24.

Rep rows 1 to 24 from Chart once more, then rows 1 to 16 once more.

His Version

Using size 3 (3.25mm) needles cast on 177 sts.

Rib row 1 [RS] P2, * k4, [p2, k3] twice, p2, k4, [p3, k3] twice, p3 *, rep from * to * 4 times more.

Rib row 2 * K3, [p3, k3] twice, p4, k2, [p3, k2] twice, p4 *, rep from * to * 4 times more, k2.

Rib row 3 P2, * C4B, [p2, k3] twice, p2, C4B, [p3, k3] twice, p3 *, rep from * to * 4 times more.

Rib row 4 As row 2.

These 4 rows set the patt.

Work a further 12 rows.

Change to size 6 (4mm) needles and cont in patt from Chart.

Row 1 P2, [work across Row 1 of 35-st patt rep of Chart] 5 times.

Row 2 [Work across Row 2 of 35-st patt rep of Chart] 5 times, k2.

These 2 rows set Chart for the 24-row rep and rev st st.

Cont in patt from Chart row 3 to end of Chart row 24.

Rep rows 1 to 24 from Chart once more, then rows 1 to 16 once more.

Shape top (both versions)

Row 1 P2, [k4, p2tog, patt 8, p2tog, k4, p2(3)tog, patt 9, p2(3)tog] 5 times. *147 sts.*

Row 2 Patt to end.

Row 3 P2, [C4Bdec, p1, patt 8, p1, C4Bdec, p1, patt 9, p1] 5 times. *127 sts.*

Row 4 Patt to end.

Row 5 P2, [Tw2R, p1, patt 8, p1, Tw2R, p1, patt 9, p1] 5 times. *127 sts.*

Row 6 Patt to end.

Row 7 P2, [Tw2R, p1, p2tog, patt 4, p2tog, p1, Tw2R, p1, k3, C6Bdec, p1] 5 times. *102 sts.*

Row 8 Patt to end.
Row 9 P2, [Tw2R, p2, C4Bdec, p2, Tw2R, p1, k6, p1] 5 times. *92 sts.*
Row 10 Patt to end.
Row 11 P2, [Tw2R, p2tog, Tw2R, p2tog, Tw2R, p1, C4B, k2tog, p1] 5 times. *77 sts.*
Row 12 * K1, [P2tog] 4 times, [k1, p2tog], twice; rep from * 4 times more, k2tog. *46 sts.*
Row 13 [K2tog] 23 times. *23 sts.*
Row 14 [P2tog] 11 times. p1. *12 sts.*
Break off yarn, thread through rem sts and fasten off.

FINISHING
Join seam. Make a pompon and attach to top.

HER HAT

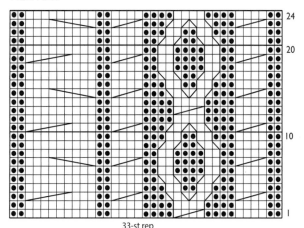

33-st rep

HIS HAT

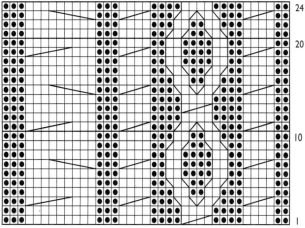

35-st rep

ABBREVIATIONS
C3R Slip next st on cable needle and hold at back of work, k2, then p1 from cable needle.
C3L Slip next 2 sts on cable needle and hold at front of work, p1, then k2 from cable needle.
C4B Slip next 2 sts on cable needle and hold at back of work, k2, then k2 from cable needle.
C4Bdec Slip next 2 sts on cable needle and hold at back of work, [k next st on left hand needle tog with first st on cable needle] twice, 2 sts dec.
C6B Slip next 3 sts on cable needle and hold at back of work, k3, then k3 from cable needle.
C6Bdec Slip next 3 sts on cable needle and hold at back of work, [k next st on left hand needle tog with 1st st on cable needle] 3 times, 3 sts dec.
C6F Slip next 3 sts on cable needle and hold at front of work, k3, then k3 from cable needle.
Tw2R K into front of 2nd st on left hand needle, then k into 1st st and slip both sts off needle tog.
See also page 127.

KEY

☐ RS, K WS, P		C3L
⚫ RS, P WS, K		C4B
		C6B
C3R		C6F

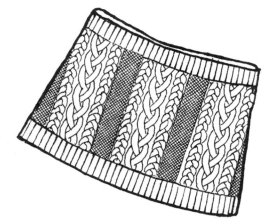

SIZE
Approx. 32½in (83cm) around by 22in (56cm) deep.

YARN

5 x 1¾oz/50g balls of Rowan Softyak DK in Driftwood 244.
CYCA#3

NEEDLES
Circular size 6 (4mm) knitting needle.
Cable needle.

GAUGE
22 sts and 30 rows to 4in/10cm square over st st using size 6 (4mm) needles.
32 sts and 30 rows to 4in/10cm square over cable patt using size 6 (4mm) needles.

NOTE: When working from Chart, read Chart from right to left on every round.

DEEP ARAN COWL**

TO MAKE
Using size 6 (4mm) circular needle cast on 264 sts.
Work in rounds.
Round 1 P2, * C4B, k2, p3, [k2, p2] twice, k2, p3, rep from * to last 20 sts, C4B, k2, p3, [k2, p2] twice, k2, p1.
Round 2 P2, * k6, p3, [k2, p2] twice, k2, p3, rep from * to last 20 sts, k6, p3, [k2, p2] twice, k2, p1.
Round 3 P2, * k2, C4F, p3, [k2, p2] twice, k2, p3, rep from * to last 20 sts, k2, C4F, p3, [k2, p2] twice, k2, p1.
Round 4 As round 2.
These 4 rounds set the patt.
Work a further 8 rounds.
Cont in patt from Chart.
Round 1 [Work across Chart Round 1 of 44-st patt rep] 6 times.
This round sets the main 8-row patt rep.
Cont in patt until work measures 10in/25cm from cast-on edge.
Round 1 (dec) [Patt 35, work 3 tog, patt 6] 6 times. *252 sts.*
Cont in patt until work measures 12in/30cm from cast on edge.
Round 2 (dec) [Patt 36, work 3 tog, patt 3] 6 times. *240 sts.*
Cont in patt until work measures 14in/35cm from cast on edge.
Round 3 (dec) [Patt 35, work 3 tog, patt 2] 6 times. *228 sts.*
Cont in patt until work measures 15¾in/40cm from cast-on edge, ending with Round 2 of patt.

Round 4 (dec) [P2tog, patt 6, p2tog, patt 12, p2tog, patt 6, p2tog, patt 6]
6 times. *204 sts.*
Work 2 rounds.
Next round * P1, patt 6, p2, [k2, p2] 3 times, patt 6, p2, k3, p2tog; rep from * 5
times. *198 sts.*
Work a further 11 rounds in cable and rib patt as set.
Bind off in patt.

ABBREVIATIONS
C4R Slip next st on cable
needle and hold at back
of work, k3, then p1 from
cable needle.
C4L Slip next 3 sts on
cable needle and hold at
front of work, p1, then k3
from cable needle.
C4B Slip next 2 sts on
cable needle and hold at
back of work, k2, then k2
from cable needle.
C4F Slip next 2 sts on
cable needle and hold at
front of work, k2, then k2
from cable needle.
C6B Slip next 3 sts on
cable needle and hold at
back of work, k3, then k3
from cable needle.
C6F Slip next 3 sts on a
cable needle and leave at
front of work, k3, then k3
from cable needle.
See also page 127.

KEY
☐ K
⊙ P
C4R
C4L
C6B
C6F
C4B
C4F

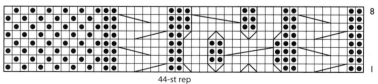

44-st rep

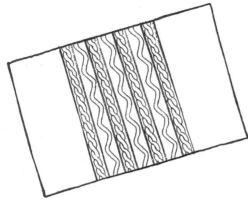

RECTANGULAR ARAN PILLOW**

BACK
Using size 5 (3.75mm) needles cast on 108 sts.
Beg with a k row, work 84 rows in st st.
Bind off.

FRONT
Using size 5 (3.75mm) needles cast on 108 sts.
K 1 row.
Inc row P34, [m1, p3] 13 times, m1, p35. *122 sts.*
Work in patt.
Row 1 K31, work across Row 1 of Chart, k31.
Row 2 P31, work across Row 2 of Chart, p31.
These 2 rows set the position for the 24-row cable panel and form the st st to the side.
Work a further 78 rows.
Dec row K34, [k2tog, k2] 13 times, k2tog, k34. *108 sts.*
P 1 row.
Bind off.

FINISHING
With right sides together, sew the back to the front along 3 sides.
Insert the pillow form and join the remaining seam.

SIZE
19in (48cm) wide by 11in (28cm) deep to fit a pillow form 19½in (50cm) wide by 12in (30cm) deep.

YARN
3 x 1¾oz/50g balls of Rowan Softyak DK Heath 238. CYCA#3

NEEDLES
Pair size 5 (3.75mm) knitting needles.
Cable needle.

EXTRAS
Pillow form 19½in (50cm) wide × 30in (12cm) deep.

GAUGE
23 sts and 30 rows to 4in/10cm square over patt using size 5 (3.75mm) needles.

ABBREVIATIONS
C6B Slip next 3 sts on cable needle, hold at back of work, k3, then k3 from cable needle.
C3R Slip next st on cable needle, hold at back of work, k2, then p1 from cable needle.
C3L Slip next 2 sts on cable needle, hold at front of work, p1, then k2 from cable needle.
See also page 127.

KEY

☐ RS, K
WS, P

⊡ RS, P
WS, K

▨ C3R

◩ C3L

▥ C6B

60 sts

24

20

10

1

LONG ARAN SCARF**

TO MAKE

Using size 3 (3.25mm) needles, cast on 66 sts.

Rib row 1 (RS) Sl1p ytf, k3, p2, k2, p2, k4, p3, k3, [p2, k2] 6 times, p2, k3, p2, k2, p2, k4, p3, k4.

Rib row 2 Sl1p ytf, k6, p4, k2, p2, k2, p3, [k2, p2] 6 times, k2, p3, k3, p4, k2, p2, k6.

Rows 3 to 10 Rep rows 1 and 2 four times.

Change to size 6 (4mm) needles.

Cont in patt from Chart, repeating rows 1 to 8 until work measures 80in/203cm from cast-on edge, ending with row 8 of patt.

Change to size 3 (3.25mm) needles.

Rep Rib rows 1 and 2 five times.

Bind off in patt.

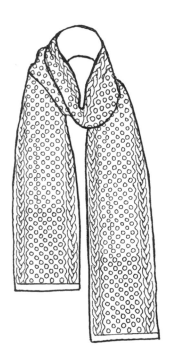

SIZE

8in (20cm) wide by 81in (206cm) long.

YARN

6 x 1¾oz/50g balls of Rowan Softyak DK Savannah 234. CYCA#3

NEEDLES

Pair each of size 3 (3.25mm) and size 6 (4mm) knitting needles. Cable needle.

GAUGE

22 sts and 30 rows to 4in/10cm over st st using size 6 (4mm) needles.

ABBREVIATIONS

C4B Slip next 2 sts on cable needle and hold at back of work, k2, then k2 from cable needle.

C4F Slip next 2 sts on cable needle and hold at front of work, k2, then k2 from cable needle.

C3R Slip next st on cable needle and hold at back of work, k2, then p1 from cable needle.

C3L Slip next 2 sts on cable needle and hold at front of work, p1, then k2 from cable needle.

T4R Slip next st on cable needle and hold at back of work, k2, then p2 from cable needle.

T4L Slip next 2 sts on cable needle and hold at front of work, p2, then k2 from cable needle.

sl1p ytf With yarn at front, slip one st purlwise.

See also page 127.

KEY

☐ RS, K
WS, P

⊡ RS, P
WS, K

▨ C3R

▨ C3L

▭ C4B

▭ C4F

▨ T4R

▨ T4L

▽ sl1p ytf
on RS & WS

66 sts

ARAN THROW**

CABLE STRIP 1 (MAKE 2)

Using size 3 (3.25mm) needles cast on 51 sts.

Rib row 1 (RS) K2, p1, k1, p2, k4, p2 * k3, p2, k2, p2, k3 *, p3, rep from * to * once more, p2, k4, p2, k1, p1, k2.

Rib row 2 [K1, p1] twice, k2, p4, k2, * p3, k2, p2, k2, p3 *, k3, rep from * to * once more, k2, p4, k2, [p1, k1] twice.

Rib row 3 K2, p1, k1, p2, C4B, p2, * k3, p2, k2, p2, k3 *, p3, rep from * to * once more, p2, C4F, p2, k1, p1, k2.

Rib row 4 As Row 2.

Rep these 4 rows, twice more.

Change to size 6 (4mm) needles and work in patt from Chart.

Chart row 1 (RS) K2, p1, k1, p2, k4, p2, k5, p1, k6, p3, k6, p1, k5, p2, k4, p2, k1, p1, k2.

Chart row 2 [K1, p1] twice, k2, p4, k2, p5, k1, p6, k3, p6, k1, p5, k2, p4, k2, [p1, k1] twice.

These 2 rows set Chart for the 40-row patt rep.

Cont in patt from Chart row 3 to end of Chart row 40.

Now rep Rows 1 to 40 from Chart, 18 times more.

Change to size 3 (3.25mm) needles.

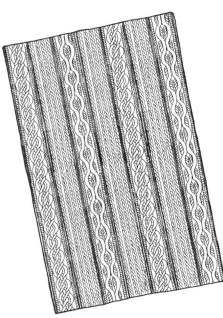

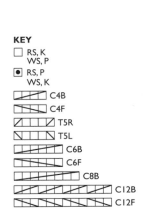

116

CABLE STRIP 1

51 sts

KEY

- ☐ RS, K
  WS, P
- ⊡ RS, P
  WS, K
- C4B
- C4F
- T5R
- T5L
- C6B
- C6F
- C8B
- C12B
- C12F

SIZE
Approx 34½in (88cm) wide × 92½in (235cm) long.

YARN
38 × 1¾oz/50g balls of Rowan Softyak DK Cream 230. CYAC#3

NEEDLES
Pair each size 3 (3.25mm) and size 6 (4mm) needles.
Cable needle.

GAUGE
22 sts and 30 rows to 4in/10cm square over st st using size 6 (4mm) needles.

ABBREVIATIONS
C4B Slip next 2 sts on cable needle, hold at back of work, k2, then k2 from cable needle.
C4F Slip next 2 sts on cable needle, hold at front of work, k2, then k2 from cable needle.
C6B Slip next 3 sts on cable needle, hold at back of work, k3, then k3 from cable needle.
C6F Slip next 3 sts on cable needle, hold at front of work, k3, then k3 from cable needle.
C12B Slip next 6 sts on cable needle, hold at back of work, k6, then k6 from cable needle.
C12F Slip next 6 sts on cable needle, hold at front of work, k6, then k6 from cable needle.
C8B Slip next 4 sts on cable needle, hold at back of work, k4, then k4 from cable needle.
T5R Slip next st on cable needle, hold at back of work, k4, then p1 from cable needle.
T5L Slip next 4 sts on cable needle, hold at front of work, p1, then k4 from cable needle.
See also page 127.

CABLE STRIP 2

50 sts

§

117

Now rep Rib rows 1 to 4, 3 times.
Bind off in patt.

CABLE STRIP 2 (MAKE 3)
Using size 3 (3.25mm) needles cast on 50 sts.
Rib row 1 (RS) K2, p1, k1, p2, [k2, p2] 10 times, k1, p1, k2.
Rib row 2 [K1, p1] twice, k2, [p2, k2] 10 times, [p1, k1] twice. Rep these 2 rows, 5 more times.
Change to size 6 (4mm) needles and work in patt from Chart.
Chart row 1 (RS) K2, p1, k1, p2, [k8, p2] 4 times, k1, p1, k2.
Chart row 2 [K1, p1] twice, k2, [p8, k2] 4 times, [p1, k1] twice.
These 2 rows set Chart for the 40-row patt rep.
Cont in patt from Chart row 3 to end of Chart row 40.
Now rep rows 1 to 40 from Chart, 18 times more.
Change to size 3 (3.25mm) needles.
Now rep Rib rows 1 and 2, 6 times.
Bind off in patt.

CABLE STRIP 3 (MAKE 2)
Using size 3 (3.25mm) needles cast on 48 sts.
Rib row 1 (RS) K2, p1, k1, p2, k4, p2, k3, p2, [k2, p2] 4 times, k3, p2, k4, p2, k1, p1, k2.

CABLE STRIP 3

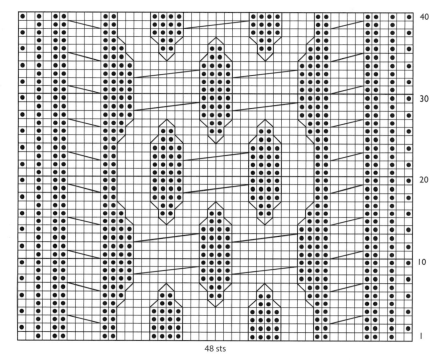

48 sts

Rib row 2 [K1, p1] twice, k2, p4, k2, p3, k2, [p2, k2] 4 times, p3, k2, p4, k2, [p1, k1] twice.

Rib row 3 K2, p1, k1, p2, C4B, p2, k3, p2, [k2, p2] 4 times, k3, p2, C4F, p2, k1, p1, k2.

Rib row 4 As Row 2.

Rep these 4 rows, twice more.

Change to size 6 (4mm) needles and work in patt from Chart.

Chart row 1 (RS) K2, p1, k1, [p2, k4] twice, p4, k8, p4, [k4, p2] twice, k1, p1, k2.

Chart row 2 [K1, p1] twice, [k2, p4] twice, k4, p8, k4, [p4, k2] twice, [p1, k1] twice.

These 2 rows set Chart for the 40-row patt rep.

Cont in patt from Chart row 3 to end of Chart row 40.

Now rep rows 1 to 40 from Chart, 18 times more.

Change to size 3 (3.25mm) needles.

Now rep Rib rows 1 to 4, 3 times

Bind off in patt.

FINISHING

Join strips together in following formation: 1, 2, 3, 2, 1, 2, 3 matching cast-on and bound-off edges, and using a neat mattress or slip stitch to join the garter stitch edges.

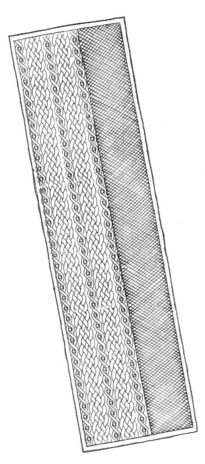

ARAN WRAP**

TO MAKE

Using size 3 (3.25mm) needles cast on 137 sts.

Rib row 1 (RS) Sllp ytf, k3 * k2, p2; rep from * to last 5 sts, k5.

Rib row 2 Sllp ytf, k3 * p2, k2; rep from * to last 5 sts, pl, k4.

Repeat these 2 rows, 29 more times.

Change to size 6 (4mm) needles and work in patt from Chart.

Row 1 (RS) Sllp ytf, k3, p2 * k24, p3, C3R, pl, C3L, p3 *, rep from * to * once more, kl, [pl, kl] 26 times, k4.

Row 2 Sllp ytf, k3, pl, [kl, pl] 26 times * [k3, p2] twice, k3, p24 *, rep from * to * once more, k6.

Row 3 Sllp ytf, k3, p2, *k24, p2, C3R, p3, C3L, p2* rep from * to * once more, pl, [kl, pl] 26 times, k4.

Row 4 Sllp ytf, k4, [pl,kl] 26 times, *k2, p2, k5, p2, k2, p24*, rep from * to * once more, k6.

These 4 rows set the position for the 12-row cable panel and form the Irish seed st at side.

Cont in patt from Chart row 5 to end of Chart row 12.

Now rep Rows 1 to 12, 54 more times, then Rows 1 to 10 from Chart once.

Change to size 3 (3.25mm) needles.

Now rep Rib rows 1 and 2, 30 times.

Bind off in patt.

SIZE
Wrap measures approx. 17¾in (45cm) wide × 83in (210cm) long.

YARN
13 × 1¾oz/50g balls of Rowan Softyak DK Taupe 245. CYCA#3

NEEDLES
Pair each size 3 (3.25mm) and size 6 (4mm) needles.
Cable needle.

GAUGE
30 sts and 34 rows to 4in/10cm square over pattern st using size 6 (4mm) needles.

ABBREVIATIONS

C8B Slip next 4 sts on cable needle and hold at back of work, k4, then k4 from cable needle.

C8F Slip next 4 sts on cable needle and hold at back front of work, k4, then k4 from cable needle.

T5B Slip next 3 sts on cable needle and hold at back of work, k2, then slip center st back onto left hand needle, p this st; then k2 from cable needle.

C3R Slip next st on cable needle and hold at back of work, k2, then p1 from cable needle.

C3L Slip next 2 sts on cable needle and hold at front of work, p1, then k2 from cable needle.

Make Bobble [k1, yfwd, k1] in next st, turn and p3, turn and k3, turn and p3, turn and sl1k, k2tog, psso. Bobble completed.

See also page.127.

KEY

☐ RS, K
  WS, P

⊡ RS, P
  WS, K

◪ C3R

◩ C3L

▱ T5B

▱ C8B

▱ C8F

■ Make Bobble

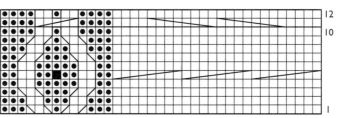

37-st rep

USEFUL INFORMATION

CABLE PATTERNS AND CHARTS

The key point to bear in mind with cable patterns is that the cable stitches have to stand out from the rest of the knitting. For this reason, if the cable stitches are to be in stockinette stitch – alternating knit (right side) and purl (wrong side) rows – then the background for these stitches would need to be in a different pattern. The most commonly used background pattern for cables is reversed stockinette stitch. What this means is that the usual right or wrong side of the pattern is reversed. In reverse stockinette stitch, the purl row is the **right side** row, and the knit row the **wrong side** row.

HOW BASIC CABLE STITCH PATTERNS ARE WRITTEN

The stitch pattern for a basic cable is expressed in the number of stitches you twist backwards and forwards (which are then split down into the number of stitches you hold on the cable needle), and the number of rows involved in each repeat. The pattern can either be written out or shown in a chart using symbols for the different stitches (see opposite), or the pattern can be a mixture of a written element for the general knitting pattern information and a chart used just for the cable panel or panels. Some people find it easier to follow a written pattern and others find it easier to follow a chart, but you should be able to do both. You will always find a note as to what special abbreviations have been used in the pattern and there will be a key to a chart where there is one. **It is essential that you always read this carefully.**

Each cable pattern abbreviation will list the number of front and/or back-cable stitches you need to work to create the cable design. The word **C** comes first, denoting cable or cross, followed by the number of stitches in the cable (say **4**, **6** or **8**, for example), followed by **B** or **F,** indicating whether the cable is worked at the **back** or **front** (i.e. the stitches are held to the back or front of the work). If the pattern requires a 6-st wide **back** cable, it will be given as **C6B.** This will mean slipping the first 3 sts of the 6 sts of the cable panel on to the cable needle and holding them at the **back** of the work while the next 3 sts are knitted, before the 3 sts on the cable needle are knitted off. For a 6-st wide forward cable **(C6F),** the same order as for C6B applies, but the stitches are held at the **front** of the work while being knitted off.

Holding the stitches at the back or front of the work will determine the way the cable twists. A back cable will lean from lower left to upper right (right leaning) while a front cable will lean from lower right to upper left (left leaning).

Below Two basic knit stitch cables on a reversed stockinette stitch background. The bottom left cable is a 4-st forward cable (C4F) while the bottom right cable is a thicker 6-st back cable (C6B). Both are knitted in Rowan Hemp Tweed.

122

READING A CABLE PATTERN CHART

At first, reading from a chart may appear very confusing but once you understand how the symbols work and how to read the rows, then it becomes clear and simple.

A chart is read exactly as the knitting is worked: from the **bottom** to the **top** of the chart, going from **right** to **left** of the chart on right-side (**RS**) rows and from **left** to **right** of the chart on wrong-side (**WS**) rows. (Note: The only exception is when you work in rounds, in which each row (or round) is read from right to left).

Each **small square** represents **"one"** stitch and all rows are shown on the chart as they appear from the right side (**RS**) of the knitting.

The numbers at the right-hand edge of the chart are the row numbers.

Chart repeats

Sometimes the chart is for a portion of the pattern only. If the pattern asks you to work from the chart for a repeated number of rows, then after the last row at the top of the chart has been worked, you begin again at the bottom with Row 1 working from the right side of the chart to the left side. The number of rows of the repeat will be marked at the side of the chart. Sometimes the pattern asks you to repeat a specific number of stitches and the number of the stitches in the repeat will be marked beneath the chart.

Symbols used for background stitches

Most of the patterns in this book are worked on a reversed stockinette stitch background, in which the purl side is the right side (in normal stockinette stitch it would be the wrong side). So, for example, the large black dot on the charts (ie the cable background) featured in this book always mean a purl stich on the right side; therefore the large black dot squares mean that you purl these stitches on the RS and knit them on the WS, as stated in the key to chart. A blank square will mean the opposite: knit on the RS, and purl on the WS.

Symbols used for basic cables

The basic knit cables (as in the **Cable Knits** section of this book) are represented by a slanting, "slash" symbol and always worked on a RS row. As each chart square represents a stitch, the number of squares the slash crosses shows the number of stitches in the cable twist. The angle of the slash from bottom right to top left in this book represents a forward cable while the angle of the slash from bottom left to top right indicates a back cable. In both cases, the number of stitches that the "slash" symbol crosses represents the number of stitches being cabled, as explained in the key to chart. Where the stitches involved in the cable twist cover multiple squares (eg C12B, C12F), the slash will be repeated as two pairs of 6 squares.

Below The cable panel charts (below) with their key, (bottom) for an alternating 6-st front and back "wave" cable (as shown in the Wave Cable Cardigan on page 32) on a reversed stockinette stitch background with 2 sts either side of the cable pattern. The cable repeats over 12 rows, as marked on the side of the chart. The sts marked below the chart indicate the cable panel width.

Left front

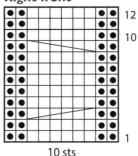

10 sts

Right front

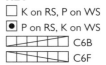

10 sts

123

KEY

☐ K on RS, P on WS
⬛ P on RS, K on WS
▭ C6B
▭ C6F

CABLES ENDING R OR L (KNIT AND PURL STITCHES CROSSED BACK OR FORWARD)

In the **Aran Knits** section of this book pattern, you will find cables that involve crossing knit over purl stitches (as in the sample shown below). In the patterns for these, the slash symbol **C** – indicating cable or cross – remains the same as in the basic cable but the direction of the slash will be indicated by **R** (crossing right) or **L** (crossing left). The number in between the C and the R or the C and the L indicates the number of stitches in the cables. Unlike the basic cable, you will see a blank square or squares **between** the slashed squares in the symbols for a crossed right or crossed left cable. For example, a C3R cable – i.e. cross 3 stitches right – will have a diagonal, right-leaning **s**lash in the first square, then a blank second square, then finally a right-leaning diagonal slash in the third square; a C3L cable – i.e. cross 3 sts left – will have a diagonal, left-leaning, slash in the first square, then a blank, second square, then finally a left-leaning diagonal slash in the third square, as shown in the key to the chart below.

Again, for cable symbols ending R or L you need to check the abbreviations listed with each pattern, which will explain which sts you need to knit and purl for an R- or L-ending cable. In order to accommodate the many different patterns, further symbols are used to explain the different knit and purl combinations they include. Pattern writers vary in the abbreviations they use, so in some patterns C5R/C5L might be written as Cr5R/Cr5L or as CR5R/C5RL, for example.

Always check the key to the chart carefully to make sure you have associated the symbols used in that pattern with the abbreviations listed for it.

Below An Open Cable (as used in the Aran scarf on p. 66) includes a C3R and a C3L cable, as well as a basic C4B cable. The chart and the key for this cable are shown below.

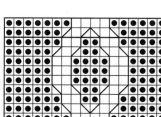

18 sts

KEY

☐ RS, K
WS, P

⊡ RS, P
WS, K

◹◺ C3R

◸◹ C3L

C4B

124

If you are new to knitting a cable pattern you may find using a cable needle a bit awkward at first. However, it is surprising how quickly you adapt. As a cable design is like a rope, it is made up of a lot of repeating cable twists. By the time you have worked a few repeats, you will find it becomes much easier, so do your practice swatches with at least three or four repeats.

Using a cranked cable needle

If you are a novice at knitting cables, it usually helps to use a cranked cable needle (the double-pointed needle with the bracket shape in the middle) rather than a straight one because it is much harder to inadvertently drop the stitches off the cranked one by mistake, particularly if your knitting tension is on the loose side. Remember, too, that your cable needle must be very similar in size to the knitting needles you are using. If it is too small, that would cause the stitches to slip off easily, and if too large, you would struggle to knit them off. And the subsequent changes in tension can create ragged edges to the cable pattern.

The bracket shape of the cranked cable needle prevents the stitches from slipping off the needle inadvertently.

Slipping stitches onto a cable needle and knitting them off

Another issue for novices is being aware how you slip the stitches on to the cable needle and then knit them off. You must knit the stitches off the cable needle in the order you slipped them onto it. This is why you need a double-pointed needle to hold them. Because, before you knit them off, you have to slide the stitches to the other end of the double-pointed needle so you are knitting off the very first stitch you slipped on. If you are using a cranked cable needle, slip the stitches **purlwise** onto it and then push them into the central cranked part of the cable needle while the needle is held at the front (forward cable) or a the back (back cable). Only slide them to the other end of the cable needle when you are ready to knit them off. Make sure you also push the stitches on the working needles reasonably close to the tips so that you are not pulling the yarn unnecessarily. You may find your tension becomes a bit tight as you knit stitches on and off the cable needle, so try to loosen this a little.

125

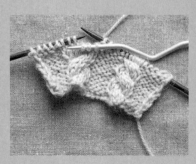

The stitches are slipped **purlwise** off the left knitting needle using the left tip of the cable needle.

They are then pushed to the cranked section of the needle while being held at the back or front.

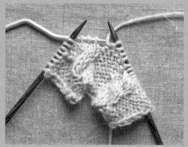

The stitches are then pushed to the **right** tip of the cable needle to knit them off with the right needle.

GENERAL INFORMATION

GAUGE

Gauge controls both the shape and size of your knitting, so any variation, however slight, can distort the measurements of the finished piece of knitting. To check your gauge, knit a square in the pattern stitch and/or stockinette stitch of perhaps 5–10 more stitches and 5–10 more rows than those given in the gauge note. Press the finished square under a damp cloth and mark out a central 4in/10cm square area with pins. If you have more stitches to the 4in/10cm area than the given gauge, knit it again using thicker needles. If you have fewer stitches than the given tension, knit it again using finer needles. Once you have achieved the correct gauge, your project will be knitted correctly to the measurements given.

FINISHING METHODS

Pressing

Block out each piece of knitting by pinning it on a board to the correct measurements in the pattern. Then lightly press it according to the ball band instructions, omitting any ribbed areas. Take special care to press the edges, as this makes sewing up easier and neater. If you cannot press the fabric, then cover the knitted fabric with a damp cloth and allow it to stand for a couple of hours. Darn in all ends neatly along the selvedge edge or a color join.

Stitching seams

When you stitch the pieces together, remember to match any areas of texture carefully where they meet and use the yarn from the pattern. Using a special seam stitch called mattress stitch (where you pick up a stitch from each side to be joined) creates the neatest flattest seam. Once all the seams are complete, press the seams and hems. Lastly, sew on the buttons to correspond with the positions of the buttonholes.

YARNS

The following Rowan yarns have been used in this book:

Rowan Hemp Tweed

This is a blend of 75 percent wool and 25 percent hemp. Hemp fiber is resistant to stretching so does not distort with use and naturally softens with wear. Specification: 1¾oz/50g balls; 104yd/95m per ball; 19sts and 25 rows to 4in/10cm square using size 7 (4.5mm) needles.

Rowan Softyak DK

This is a blend of 76 percent cotton, 15 percent yak and 9 percent nylon. It has a very soft handle. Specification: 1¾oz/50g balls; 147yd/135m per ball; 22 sts and 30 rows to 4in/10cm using size 6 (4mm) needles.

SKILLS RATINGS

The patterns in this book have been given the following ratings according to the level of skill required:

* easy cable stitch pattern/ pattern without shaping.

** easy cable stitch pattern with shaping/easy Aran stitch pattern without shaping.

*** easy Aran stitch pattern with shaping.

Abbreviations

(see individual patterns for special cable abbreviations)

alt	alternate	sk2po	sl 1, knit 2 together, pass slipped stitch over
approx	approximately		
beg	begin(s)(ning)	sl 1	slip one st
cm	centimeters	sl1k	Slip one stitch knitwise (with yarn in back of work)
cont	continu(e)(ing)		
dec	decreas(e)(ing)		
foll(s)	follow(s)(ing)	sl1p	Slip one stitch purlwise (with yarn in front of work)
g	gram		
g-st	garter stitch		
in	inch(es)	sl2k	Slip two sts knitwise
inc	increas(e)(ing)	ssk	Slip next 2 sts singly to RH needle knitwise, insert tip of LH needle through front loops of both sts and k together.
k	knit		
k2tog	knit next 2 sts together		
k3tog	knit next 3 sts together		
mm	millimeters		
M1	make one st by picking up horizontal loop before next st and knitting into back of it	st(s)	stitch(es)
		st st	stockinette stitch (1 row k, 1 row purl)
patt	pattern	tbl	through back of loop(s)
p	purl	tog	together
psso	pass slipped stitch over	WS	wrong side
p2tog	purl next 2 sts together	yd	yard(s)
rem	remain(s)(ing)	yf	yarn forward
rep	repeat	yo	yarn over
RS	right side	ytf	with yarn to front
skpo	sl 1, k1, pass slipped stitch over	ytb	with yarn to back
		[ ]/*	repeat instructions within square brackets or between asterisks

127

ACKNOWLEDGMENTS

A big, big thank you to the following: Steven and Susan for the wonderful photography, art direction, styling and graphics; Penny Hill for pattern writing and knitting, and Frances Jago also for knitting; Jill Gray and Marilyn Wilson for diligent checking; Anne Wilson and Steve Jacobson, for their diagrams; Laure Gautier, Juliette Rebiere-Olleans and Harriet Taylor for modelling for us with such aplomb; and, of course, to the entire team at Rowan for their continuing support.

STOCKISTS

AUSTRALIA Australian Country Spinners, Pty Ltd, Level 7, 409 St. Kilda Road, Melbourne Vic 3004. **tel** 03 9380 3888 **fax** 03 9820 0989 **email** customerservice@auspinners.com.au

AUSTRIA MEZ Harlander GmbH, Schulhof 6, 1. Stock, 1010 Wien, Austria **tel** + 00800 26 27 28 00 **fax** (00) 49 7644 802-133 **email** verkauf.harlander@mezcrafts.com

BELGIUM MEZ crafts Belgium NV, c/o MEZ GmbH, Kaiserstr.1, 79341 Kenzingen, Germany **tel** 0032 (0) 800 77 89 2 **fax** 00 49 7644 802 133 **email** sales.be-nl@mezcrafts.com

BULGARIA MEZ Crafts Bulgaria EOOD, 7 Magnaurska Shkola Str, BG-1784 Sofia, Bulgaria **tel** (+359 2) 976 77 41 **fax** (+359 2) 976 77 20 **email** office.bg@mezcrafts.com

CANADA Sirdar USA Inc. 406 20th Street SE, Hickory, North Carolina, USA 28602 **tel** 828 404 3705 **fax** 828 404 3707 **email** sirdarusa@sirdar.co.uk

CHINA Commercial agent Mr Victor Li, c/o MEZ GmbH Germany, Kaiserstr. 1, 79341 Kenzingen / Germany **tel** (86-21) 13816681825 **email** victor.li@mezcrafts.com

CHINA SHANGHAI YUJUN CO.,LTD., Room 701 Wangjiao Plaza, No.175 Yan'an (E), 200002 Shanghai, China **tel** +86 2163739785 **email** jessechang@vip.163.com

CYPRUS MEZ Crafts Bulgaria EOOD, 7 Magnaurska Shkola Str., BG-1784 Sofia, Bulgaria **tel** (+359 2) 976 77 41 **fax** (+359 2) 976 77 20 **email** marketing.cy@mezcrafts.com

CZECH REPUBLIC Coats Czecho s.r.o.Staré Mesto 246 569 32 **tel** (420) 461616633 **email** galanterie@coats.com

DENMARK Carl J. Permin A/S Egegaardsvej DK-2610 Rødovre **tel** (45) 36 72 12 00 **email** permin@permin.dk

ESTONIA MEZ Crafts Estonia OÜ, Ampri tee 9/4, 74001 Viimsi Harjumaa **tel** +372 630 6252 **email** info.ee@mezcrafts.com

FINLAND Prym Consumer Finland Oy, Huhtimontie 6, 04200 KERAVA **tel** +358 9 274871

FRANCE 3bcom, 35 avenue de Larrieu, 31094 Toulouse cedex 01, France **tel** 0033 (0) 562 202 096 **email** Commercial@3b-com.com

GERMANY MEZ GmbH, Kaiserstr. 1, 79341 Kenzingen, Germany **tel** 0049 7644 802 222 **email** kenzingen.vertrieb@mezcrafts.com **fax** 0049 7644 802 300

GREECE MEZ Crafts Bulgaria EOOD, 7 Magnaurska Shkola Str., BG-1784 Sofia, Bulgaria **tel** (+359 2) 976 77 41 **fax** (+359 2) 976 77 20 **email** marketing.gr@mezcrafts.com

HOLLAND G. Brouwer & Zn B.V., Oudhuijzerweg 69, 3648 AB Wilnis, Netherlands **tel** 0031 (0) 297-281 557 **email** info@gbrouwer.nl

HONG KONG East Unity Company Ltd, Unit B2, 7/F., Block B, Kailey Industrial Centre, 12 Fung Yip Street, Chai Wan **tel** (852)2869 7110 **email** eastunityco@yahoo.com.hk

ICELAND Carl J. Permin A/S Egegaardsvej DK-2610 Rødovre **tel** (45) 36 72 12 00 **email** permin@permin.dk

ITALY Mez Cucirini Italy Srl, Viale Sarca, 223, 20126 MILANO **tel** 0039 0264109080 **email** servizio.clienti@mezcrafts.com **fax** 02 64109080

JAPAN Hobbyra Hobbyre Corporation, 23-37, 5-Chome, Higashi-Ohi, Shinagawa-Ku, 1400011 Tokyo. **tel** +81334721104 Daidoh International, 3-8-11 Kudanminami Chiyodaku, Hiei Kudan Bldg 5F, 1018619 Tokyo **tel** +81-3-3222-7076 **fax** +81-3-3222-7066

KOREA My Knit Studio, 3F, 144 Gwanhun-Dong, 110-300 Jongno-Gu, Seoul **tel** 82-2-722-0006 **email** myknit@myknit.com

LATVIA Coats Latvija SIA, Mukusalas str. 41 b, Riga LV-1004 **tel** +371 67 625173 **fax** +371 67 892758 **email** info.latvia@coats.com

LEBANON y.knot, Saifi Village, Mkhalissiya Street 162, Beirut **tel** (961) 1 992211 **fax** (961) 1 315553 **email** y.knot@cyberia.net.lb

LITHUANIA MEZ Crafts Lithuania UAB, A. Juozapaviciaus str. 6/2, LT-09310 Vilnius **tel** +370 527 30971 **fax** +370 527 2305 **email** info.lt@mezcrafts.com

LUXEMBOURG Coats N.V., c/o Coats GmbH, Kaiserstr.1, 79341 Kenzingen, Germany **tel** 00 49 7644 802 222 **fax** 00 49 7644 802 133 **email** sales.coatsninove@coats.com

MEXICO Estambres Crochet SA de CV, Aaron Saenz 1891-7Pte, 64650 MONTERREY **tel** +52 (81) 8335-3870 **email** abremer@redmundial.com.mx

NEW ZEALAND ACS New Zealand, P.O Box 76199, Northwood, Christchurch, New Zealand **tel** 64 3 323 6665 **fax** 64 3 323 6660 **email** lynn@impactmg.co.nz

NORWAY Carl J. Permin A/S Egegaardsvej 28 DK-2610 Rødovre **tel** (45) 36 72 12 00 **email** permin@permin.dk

PORTUGAL Mez Crafts Portugal, Lda – Av. Vasco da Gama, 774 - 4431-059 V.N, Gaia, Portugal **tel** 00 351 223 770700 **email** sales.iberia@mezcrafts.com

RUSSIA Family Hobby, 124683, Moskau, Zelenograd, Haus 1505, Raum III **tel** 007 (499) 270-32-47 Handtel. 007 916 213 74 04 **email** tv@fhobby.ru **web** www.family-hobby.ru

SINGAPORE Golden Dragon Store, BLK 203 Henderson Rd #07-02, 159546 Henderson Indurstrial Park Singapore **tel** (65) 62753517 **fax** (65) 62767112 **email** gdscraft@hotmail.com

SLOVAKIA MEZ Crafts Slovakia, s.r.o. Seberíniho 1, 821 03 Bratislava, Slovakia **tel** +421 2 32 30 31 19 **email** galanteria@mezcrafts.com

SOUTH AFRICA Arthur Bales LTD, 62 4th Avenue, Linden 2195 **tel** (27) 11 888 2401 **fax** (27) 11 782 6137 **email** arthurb@new.co.za

SPAIN MEZ Fabra Spain S.A, Avda Meridiana 350, pta 13 D, 08027 Barcelona **tel** +34 932908400 **fax** +34 932908409 **email** atencion.clientes@mezcrafts.com

SWEDEN Carl J. Permin A/S Egegaardsvej 28 DK-2610 Rødovre **tel** (45) 36 72 12 00 **email** permin@permin.dk

SWITZERLAND MEZ Crafts Switzerland GmbH, Stroppelstrasse20, 5417 Untersiggenthal, Switzerland **tel** +41 00800 2627 2800 **fax** 0049 7644 802 133 **email** verkauf.ch@mezcrafts.com

TURKEY MEZ Crafts Tekstil A.S, Kavacık Mahallesi, Ekinciler Cad. Necip Fazıl Sok. No.8 Kat: 5, 34810 Beykoz / Istanbul **tel** +90 216 425 88 10

TAIWAN Cactus Quality Co Ltd, 7FL-2, No. 140, Sec.2 Roosevelt Rd, Taipei, 10084 Taiwan, R.O.C. **tel** 00886-2-23656527 **fax** 886-2-23656503 **email** cqcl@ms17.hinet.net

THAILAND Global Wide Trading, 10 Lad Prao Soi 88, Bangkok 10310 **tel** 00 662 933 9019 **fax** 00 662 933 9110 **email** global.wide@yahoo.com

USA Sirdar USA Inc. 406 20th Street SE, Hickory, North Carolina, USA 28602 **tel** 828 404 3705 **fax** 828 404 3707 **email** sirdarusa@sirdar.co.uk

UK Mez Crafts U.K, 17F Brooke's Mill, Armitage Bridge, Huddersfield, HD4 7NR **web** www.mezcrafts.com **tel** 01484 950630

For more stockists in all countries please log on to
www.knitrowan.com